Manufacturing Consensus

MANUFACTURING CONSENSUS

UNDERSTANDING PROPAGANDA
IN THE ERA OF AUTOMATION
AND ANONYMITY

• • •

SAMUEL WOOLLEY

Yale

UNIVERSITY PRESS

New Haven and London

Published with assistance from the foundation established in memory of Henry Weldon Barnes of the Class of 1882, Yale College.

Yale University Press books may be purchased in quantity for educational, business, or promotional use. For information, please e-mail sales.press@yale.edu (U.S. office) or sales@yaleup.co.uk (U.K. office).

Set in Gotham and Adobe Garamond type by Newgen North America.
Printed in the United States of America.

Library of Congress Control Number: 2022934322
ISBN 978-0-300-25123-4 (hardcover : alk. paper)

A catalogue record for this book is available from the British Library.

This paper meets the requirements of ANSI/NISO Z39.48-1992 (Permanence of Paper).

10 9 8 7 6 5 4 3 2 1

To my mom and dad

Contents

Preface

This is a book about people. Specifically, it's a book about people who use new, emerging, or limited-access technologies in attempts to get what they want. Sometimes, these people are using automated profiles on social media—social bots—in order to make money. These "bot builders" understand that the more traction a post gets, and the more "people" click on the link in that post, the more eyeballs they get on web advertisements and the more cash they rake in. In other cases, the digital propagandists I talked to are people who understand enough about the inner workings of the internet that they can manipulate the system for political ends. They use a variety of strategies and tools—bots and other forms of inorganic web traffic, such as sockpuppets or coordinated armies of likeminded or paid people—in order to spread a particular message.

This isn't a book about counting the numbers—about figuring out how many Twitter accounts are bots, or how much a particular election was influenced by propaganda, or even how many people (and countries) are engaging in this type of influencing. There is certainly merit in that work, but it's not my work. I think this is important to say because I often get mistaken for a computer scientist, a network scientist, or a specialist in quantitative methods. This is probably because my work focuses on the technical world, and many people assume that my research itself will therefore be technical and numbers-driven. But my focus, while empirical, is on describing the novel ways people use technology, and on illuminating how these uses are tied to larger cultural phenomena. Therefore, I make use of fieldwork and the tools of ethnography, research techniques that are centered on *people*. I spend a lot of time talking to people. I not only formally interview them but also have all manner of more causal interactions based around their work and interests. I watch people do what they do, record it, analyze it in comparison to similar cases, and write it up.

So, this book is just that—a story of compiled notes from the field. It is about the people who make, build, and leverage technology in attempts to manipulate public opinion. It's about their particular uses of the curious and mutable tools and strategies that are constantly evolving out of the rich primordial ooze of the internet: bots, sockpuppet accounts, influencers, astroturfing, and so on. In the end, the book is about the humans experimenting with new forms of propaganda and how these new tools challenge our ideas of democratic communication. In this book, I show that our old ideas about propaganda are grounded in older technologies and media, such as radio, television, film, newspapers, and even the broadsides and pamphlets that emerged in the 1600s in the wake of the printing press. These ideas need an update. They need to incorporate novel contemporary media structures—the networked, many-to-many production culture of the internet. Perhaps more importantly, they need to grapple with the anonymity and automation the internet enables. The problem of propaganda is not just that anyone can now produce "news" or become an influencer. It is that they can also use anonymity and automation to gain a marked advantage in their communication. They can hide who is behind a given propaganda campaign. They can amplify, or suppress, particular streams of information, altering people's access to that information in explicit and implicit efforts to shape their opinions and behaviors.

I've tried to be candid and open about my own part in this story while writing this book. I firmly believe that the person doing field-work on a given topic influences and operates around the thing they are studying. By being reflexive, and reflective, I hope to make what follows more accessible, more understandable, and more accurate. Some of what appears here is vivid and raw, while other parts are theoretical, empirical, and analytic. I think all of this content has a place in qualitative work. Indeed, that's why I love it. And while this book is certainly academic, it is also meant to speak to people outside of the ivory tower—activists, journalists, policymakers, and everyday folks. I hope this book's idiosyncratic yet pragmatic approach is help-ful. Most of all, I hope you enjoy and find some use for the things you read here.

Acknowledgments

For their steady support, love, and care, I'd like to thank my family: my wife Samantha, Mom, Dad, Justin, Oliver, Basket, Mathilda, Banjo, and Charley. I'd also like to thank both of my grannies, Ann and Alwyn, for teaching us all how to persevere and have fun in the face of the pandemic and myriad other challenges. Thanks to the extended Woolley and Donaldson clans, and to the Shoreys, Westlunds, Joens, Bossengers, Gambles, and others. I couldn't do any of this without my friends—you know who you are, you rock.

Thanks to the faculty and staff at the School of Journalism and Media, the Center for Media Engagement (CME), and the Moody College of Communication at the University of Texas at Austin. I'm greatly indebted to all of my fantastic colleagues, collaborators, and friends at UT and can't think of a place I'd rather be. Thank you to my amazing, brilliant research team at the CME Propaganda Lab: Inga, Jo, Martin, Zelly, Ana, Joao, Dariya, Josh, Chenyan, Katlyn, Stu, Emily, Alexandra, Ahmer, Craig, and co. A massive thank you to Heath Sledge, editor extraordinaire, for helping me whip this manuscript into shape. I would like to acknowledge the guidance and mentorship of several great researchers, writers, and academics: Phil Howard, Talia Stroud, Jay Bernhardt, Kathleen McElroy, Benjamin Mako Hill, Gina Neff, Ryan Calo, and many others among them. Thank you to my frequent collaborators and co-conspirators Nick, Doug, Katie, Jacob, Helen, Mark, and Tim.

I am grateful to the faculty at the Department of Communication at the University of Washington, the Oxford Internet Institute at the University of Oxford, the Program for Democracy and the Internet at Stanford University, and the CITRIS and Banatao Institute at UC Berkeley. I am also thankful for fellowships at the German Marshall Fund; the Anti-Defamation League; Google's think-tank, Jigsaw; Central European University's Center for Media, Data, and Society; the Tech Policy Lab at the University of Washington; and the Institute for the Future, all of which stretched my thinking about the political use of automated technology. I developed ideas in portions of this work through feedback from several workshops, talks, and paper presentations at the Stanford Hoover Institution and Freeman Spogli Institute, the Yale Information Society Project, the Data and Society Research Institute, the Annenberg-Oxford Media Policy Summer Institute, and the Princeton Center for Information Technology Policy.

Please direct any correspondence to the School of Journalism and Media, Belo Center for New Media, Moody College of Communication, UT Austin, 300 West Dean Keeton Street, Austin, TX 78712. Parts of the research for this project were supported by grants from the U.S. National Science Foundation, the Ford Foundation, the Hewlett Foundation, the Omidyar Network, the Open Society Foundations, New Venture Fund for Communications, and the European Research Council. Any opinions, findings, and conclusions or recommendations expressed in this material are those of the author and do not reflect the views of the University of Texas at Austin or any funders.

Manufacturing Consensus

Propaganda, Social Media, and Political Bots

Introduction

Hernan is a self-professed digital "growth hacker."[1] He spends his days working on new, devious ways to market to clients online, with a focus on recruiting social media influencers to endorse particular products. His specialty—the product he most often works to promote—is politics. Specifically, he works to create authentic-looking interactions for campaigns, candidates, and causes. The key here is "authentic-*looking*." In truth, the support that Hernan drums up for his clients is anything but authentic. He is not an activist engaging in community organizing. He doesn't recruit actual organic, "grassroots" political supporters to work for a common cause. Instead, he traffics in what he calls "like exchanges" or "reaction exchanges."

Hernan, who is in his early thirties, spends most of his days staring at a computer screen in his office in Mexico City. From his chair, he recruits people across multiple social media sites to essentially rent out their profiles for money. He and his colleagues then take over the accounts of these "rising influencers," using them to like specific political content, post comments, watch video stories, and vote in online polls. Everything Hernan does is aimed at lending politicians and other clients the illusion of large-scale online support, amplifying their popularity—and artificially boosting attacks on their opposition. His goal is to manipulate social media algorithms to categorize particular people or topics as "trending," featuring the artificially boosted content and getting it in front of more and more "real" users.

Hernan thus works to create a bandwagon effect for his clients—to actually recruit more real followers or adherents who believe in these false messages, drawn in because it seems that other users are.

If Hernan's efforts seem to fall into a gray area of political marketing—and if they seem too tangled to easily identify as "inauthentic"—it is by design. Hernan is a computational propagandist, like the Russian government hackers who notoriously sought to shift public opinion during the 2016 U.S. elections. Like Hernan, the Russians used various digital tools and strategies—combinations of automated social media profiles (political bots) and fake profiles run by real people (sockpuppets)—to game social media systems. Hernan's political clients include a former Mexican presidential candidate, members of the Mexican Senate, and eight different candidates for various Mexican state governor races in 2021. Like many of his colleagues, he also does growth hacking for businesses, paying to use influencers' accounts to hype products. He operates a Twitter "phone farm" side business run by an entire team of employees, each of whom runs "hundreds" of sockpuppet accounts on the microblogging platform that interact with content and other users on behalf of clients. Unlike bot-run profiles, he claims, his thousands of phone farm accounts are difficult for Twitter to detect and delete.

A close friend of Hernan's, though, keeps his computational manipulation activities mostly focused on politics, not profit. Carlos Merlo became famous (or perhaps infamous) in Mexico for a profile BuzzFeed News wrote about him titled "Meet the 29-Year-Old Trying to Become the King of Mexican Fake News." In their introduction, the authors sum up the aspiring disinformation mogul's efforts: "Armed with millions of bots and thousands of fake Facebook pages, Carlos Merlo's digital marketing firm is trying to hijack Mexico's politics with fake news." He seems to be well on his way; Merlo claims that he successfully used thousands of bot profiles to spin the flow of information on behalf of powerful politicians during the 2018 Mexican election—all with little to no oversight from Twitter or Facebook. According to BuzzFeed, "Merlo estimates that these days, around 90 percent of all trending topics in Mexico are controlled by digital marketing firms."[2] Hernan says he has worked on multiple social media projects with Merlo but that his buddy had to go into hiding after the story about his operation ran. (According to Hernan, this has affected Merlo's business model; the two are now running a side-hustle selling face masks during the COVID-19 pandemic.) This claim is interesting, for according to an interviewee named Fausta—who specializes in tracking Mexican disinformation on social media—Merlo sought out the BuzzFeed reporters, pitching the story himself in hopes of propelling his own success.

Hernan and Merlo are just two of the many computational propagandists in Mexico, which (like India, the Philippines, and Ukraine) is home to a highly advanced market for computational propaganda. In these propaganda hubs, governments, militaries, nongovernmental organizations (NGOs), partisan groups, and even wealthy individuals can choose from an array of firms or professionals who specialize in generating manipulative online political communication campaigns. In some of these countries, such as Venezuela and Russia, the regimes operate hybrid public-commercial entities, keeping some propaganda efforts in-house while others are sold to the highest bidder. Others, like the Brazilian state, run their own internal "offices of hate." In Brazil, these are a "clandestine network of bots, businessmen and bloggers" purpose-built "to rain vitriol on all who oppose President Jair Bolsonaro."[3]

But it's not just governments and powerful political entities that leverage computational propaganda to spin information flows over social media in their favor. Just as anyone can be a "journalist" on Twitter, anyone with an internet connection can be a propagandist.

Never before have such large swaths of society been able to harness media (and the anonymity and automation tools enabled by the internet) to politically harass opponents and magnify their own political messages, many of which are rife with disinformation.

Modern Propaganda:
The Manufacture of Consensus Online

This book is an exploration of modern propaganda, illuminated by my eight years in the field studying how different people use social media as a tool in efforts to control political conversations on- and offline. Historically, propaganda meant the messages (usually untrue or slanted) that were officially spread by governments on mass media in order to sway public opinion. Nowadays, people casually throw around the term *propaganda*, stretching it into near-unrecognizability; it is often used simply to cast doubt on a political rival's communication—or indeed on any position that people disagree with. But the term has a technical meaning, one related to the flow of information. In this book, when I say *propaganda*, I mean the use of politically biased information in considered attempts to manipulate or influence the opinions and actions of individuals and, more broadly, society. These propagandistic messages sometimes contain entirely false content, but they might also harness the power of partial truths. They may be deceptive, obscuring who is behind them and what their goals are, or they may be coercive, using threats or force to get people to act. They are designed to cause attitudinal and behavioral change. However, this change need not be something as concrete as, say, getting someone to overhaul their political ideology or change their vote from one candidate to another. A great deal of propaganda is actually more focused on generating emotions, such as anger or apathy toward a given political system, in order to foment societal discontent. These types of campaigns are often more difficult to track, and many times they are deliberately constructed to hide mappable lines of cause and effect.

Crucially, contemporary coordinated and deliberate efforts to sow propaganda exist inside broader social and cultural contexts. They are often inextricable from their timing, semantic nuance (or lack thereof), and networked spread, and they are also intimately tied to both highly specific and broad systems of meaning. They are best understood in relationship to sociological circumstances. Their nature and the qualities that characterize them are, to me, more important than how many of these campaigns are occurring or how many people are participating in them. Early work on propaganda focused on ascertaining its psychological effect on individuals or small groups in controlled settings. I am less interested in this experimental approach than in propaganda's subjectivity and the way it is embedded in our contemporary world.

A few terms are central to my discussions here, and brief definitions of them will be helpful as you read the rest of this book. *Bias* means that a given political message is spread with particular political motivations in mind—with prejudice for or against specific ideas, people, or events. *Coercion* is focused on getting someone to do something via illicit means (through manipulation, violence, etc.). *Deception* is primarily about the intentions of the person spreading the message: it means that the motivations of the communication are opaque, that there is a lack of transparency about who is actually spreading a message and why. While it can also mean that the content of a given message is false—that the information provided is purposefully factually incorrect—not all factually incorrect information is deceptive; many people who spread propaganda believe that the content they are sharing is true. Messages that are simply factually incorrect are known as *misinformation*. The truth—events and ideas supported by empirically verifiable evidence—is not up for debate, but the framing of those facts is, and propaganda's framing can radically change how the reader interprets those facts. The type of propaganda messages discussed in this book are always coercive but not always deceptive.

Of course, there are other types of messaging campaigns designed to change opinions and behaviors, such as public interest campaigns to encourage people to get vaccinated or to vote—messaging campaigns that are open about their intentions. These are not the kind of propaganda I am concerned with here. Under older definitions of propaganda, such campaigns have been considered propagandistic simply because they involve top-down efforts by states or other actors to alter behaviors of the populace. This book instead focuses on other, less transparent information-oriented endeavors, and particularly those that occur over digital media channels. I am looking at those automated and anonymous propaganda offensives that aim to drum up influence by amplifying some messages and suppressing others.

Note that my definition of propaganda updates the historical definition, most of which is based on the notion that propaganda flows from the top down—from the powerful elite to ordinary people. This is not the way power—or information—necessarily flows on the internet. As my years of research among those that make and launch propaganda campaigns has shown, social media and the internet now make it possible for nearly anyone to launch fairly sophisticated, computationally enhanced propaganda campaigns. Social media has "democratized" not only the ability to spread information but also the ability to spread propaganda.[4]

On the internet, those top-down information flows are upended; the internet allows for many-to-many communication rather than one-to-many communication. This means that anyone with access to a smartphone can make news, going "viral" for capturing the first video of a newsworthy event. It also means that regular citizens have in their pockets the power to spread propaganda to millions using social media. On Twitter, research shows, lies and conspiracy spread faster, and to many more people, than truth does.[5] Today, powerful groups like governments and corporations are able to effectively leverage their superior resources—and what technology theorist Langdon Winner describes as their "more sophisticated, more ruthless" approach—to efficiently spread potent anonymous and automated propaganda.[6] But this loaded messaging from elites exists alongside (and often capitalizes on) similarly manipulative digital content from all sorts of other folks.

The kind of digital propaganda I discuss in this book is manipulative, often deceptive, and often coercive: there is no "positive propaganda" here. This is not so for previous studies of propaganda; for influential scholars of broadcast-era propaganda, including Walter Lippmann and Edward L. Bernays, propaganda is not inherently illiberal nor does it necessarily constitute "bad" political behavior.[7,8] For these pre-internet scholars, propaganda is biased, certainly, but the morality of a given strand of loaded political communication is in the eye of the beholder. In contrast, the propaganda I discuss here is necessarily illiberal, always nefarious. The influence-oriented work of various groups of political actors, from the Russian government to the United States's multifarious alt-right, is realizing social media's potential as a communication tool that can divide rather than unify. They are harnessing the many-to-many communication ecosystem to produce a massive amount of noise, confusion, and polarization in order to obscure the facts of particular events and the motivations of those who put out biased narratives. It also makes it easy for us to ignore—or never even see—"takes" that do not perfectly match our own existing worldviews.

As its title suggests, *Manufacturing Consensus* is a continuation of the sense-making work on propaganda of Lippmann and, later, Edward S. Herman and Noam Chomsky.[9,10] As Antonio Gramsci argued, those in power work to engineer assent from the public via cultural hegemony.[11] Lippmann expanded this to propaganda in his seminal work *Public Opinion*, discussing how propaganda can be used in the "manufacture of consent." Following Lippmann, Herman and Chomsky titled their own book on the subject *Manufacturing Consent*, borrowing the term to describe the ways in which the news media control production of information to engineer perceptions of current events—often at the behest of the powerful few who hold the strings of massive media companies like Disney, News Corp, and Time Warner.

In this book, I extend and amend this idea for our present moment, focusing on the manufacture not of assent or consent but of *consensus*. Propaganda has changed to take advantage of the affordances of what we call the "new" media system, ushered in by the internet, social media, and related forms of digital communication.[12] Social media in particular, with its anonymity and capacity for automation, has allowed for a substantively different form of propaganda—one where both computational tools (such as bots) and human-driven efforts (such as sockpuppets and partisan nanoinfluencers) allow various political groups to create the illusion of popular support for their ideas or candidates. In other words, these groups leverage social media and particular informational strategies—what my colleagues and I have termed *computational propaganda*—to manufacture *consensus* around ideas and people, creating "the illusion of popularity in an effort to create bandwagon support."[13] The bandwagon effect (in which people simply do what everyone else seems to be doing) works whether or not readers actively believe the information being pushed; the sheer volume of bogus information online creates the illusion of broad consensus unless users actively engage with and debunk it.[14]

Modern propaganda and its outcomes are not determined fully either by the technologies that make it possible or by the society from which it emerges, for the two are deeply intertwined. As the media ecosystem has expanded to include digital media, propaganda itself has changed to take advantage of it, for as Jacques Ellul argued, propaganda is a sociological phenomenon—a whole system of mediated control.[15] Various aspects of digital media, and particularly the tools enabled by social media, afford particular social undertakings. I use the broad definition of social media from Philip Howard and Malcolm Parks. They argue it "consists of (a) the information infrastructure and tools used to produce and distribute content that has individual value but reflects shared values; (b) the content that takes the digital form of personal messages, news, ideas, that becomes cultural products; and (c) the people, organizations, and industries that produce and consume both the tools and the content."[16] On social media platforms (by which I mean the websites themselves as well as the architectures that support them), people leverage the whole ecosystem of digital media tools to coerce others. They use humans to communicate with and control both humans and machines, and use machines to communicate to both humans and other machines. They leverage a wide variety of manipulation strategies, ranging from outright lies to selective truths.

As Yochai Benkler, Robert Faris, and Hal Roberts discuss, digital propaganda flourishes in a circular, networked media environment. They show how during the 2016 U.S. election, propaganda and disinformation spread throughout the whole media ecosystem, from digital to broadcast to print.[17] This often happens when legacy media report on successful computational propaganda campaigns, attempting to debunk them. However, these attempts simply spread the propaganda further, legitimizing it and perhaps even increasing the bandwagon effect. The people who work to manufacture consensus use every media tool across multiple social media sites like Facebook, YouTube, Twitter, Weibo, and Telegram to control information flows, and the political bias and deception embedded in the information they share are designed to circularly interact with—and inform—propaganda flowing from traditional media organizations: newspapers, television stations, radios, magazines, and the like. When traditional media rely on social media data for story leads and informational sourcing, they simply repackage (and, more dangerously, legitimize) propaganda. As Whitney Phillips notes, a mainstream media organization's decision to report on a conspiracy theory (or a mass shooter's manifesto or extremist gathering, etc.) can give "oxygen" to the person or group that perpetuated the content or act in the first place, amplifying the cause of propagandists and hate groups.[18] Indeed, such organizations often begin to sow falsehoods or hate online precisely in order to get their content into the broader media ecosystem.[19]

Core Concepts

The research and arguments in this book are born out of my long-term set of research concerns centering on computational propaganda—the use of automation and algorithms over social media to manipulate public opinion.[20] As a doctoral student, I and a small team of other researchers began working to define and understand the sociotechnical concept of computational propaganda. I researched how these various automated and algorithmic tools and strategies were being used by a wide variety of groups around the world in efforts to control the flow of political information. For the first several years, my work primarily focused on analyzing the use of political bots: automated profiles on social media employed to communicate about politics, usually run by political groups hoping to spin conversations in their favor or to frame a given situation or person in a particular light. My colleagues and I analyzed how these automated social actors were deployed around the world during elections and political crises.[21,22] Since then, my individual work has focused on conducting networked ethnographic research among the people who build, combat, and experience the propaganda campaigns waged using bots and other digital tools and tactics: industry experts, computer engineers, journalists, political campaign workers, PR consultants, and many others.[23] The insights in this book are primarily drawn from interview- and field-based work among these groups, which has taken place in various places around the world over the last eight years. To understand the ethnographic insights I offer here, we need a basic shared understanding of the technical underpinnings of the digital media systems that allow people to create and spread computational propaganda—the digital tools at the heart of propagandists' ability to spread disinformation and manipulate public opinion.

One of the key computational propaganda strategies is *automation*, which here refers to technology built to undertake particular functions with little human oversight. One example of automation is the *bot*—a software tool built to do autonomous tasks, including communicate with other users online. Bots are often core mechanisms for spreading computational propaganda. They can functionally extend the reach of a single person, allowing them to reach many more people than otherwise possible. A bot-herder controlling a set of given social media bots built to look like real human users can spread a given message one hundred or one thousand times more than they could without automation. Bots may be either mostly mechanical (they can be used to engage in simple mass copy/paste posting of the exact same content by rote) or partially human-controlled (accounts that are partially human-run and mix independent content with formulaic propagandistic content—a form of account that is much more difficult to detect). Increasingly, they can be encoded with learning and decision-making capabilities via advances in machine learning and artificial intelligence.

Another key component of computational propaganda is the *algorithms* that digital propagandists exploit. An algorithm is a defined set of procedures or instructions followed by a computer in order to solve a particular problem. Twitter's trending algorithm, for instance, determines what information is popular with users and serves that information to other users; it makes these curation decisions by analyzing the volume of content concerning a particular topic over time, with prioritization given to "sharp spikes" rather than long-term information growth.[24] Algorithms are human-designed and therefore have various types of bias hard-coded into them, but they often don't get necessary human oversight in their day-to-day operations; they are therefore relatively easy for propagandists to manipulate.

As most people know, bots—which are growing increasingly sophisticated and difficult to detect—are often used to spread manipulative political content. Recently, though, sockpuppet accounts have become almost equally common vectors for political manipulation. Sockpuppets are real people who assume false identities online. While these accounts can't amplify content as quickly or as widely as automated tools, they play a crucial role in the spread of manipulative political messaging over digital media. They are particularly successful at triggering the bandwagon effect, for people are much more willing to trust information that comes from someone they know— even those whom they only know parasocially, like an Instagram or Twitch personality—than from a stranger.[25] I have recently begun to see social media influencers with relatively small accounts being used as sockpuppets to spread political or partisan information in large-scale propaganda campaigns.[26] These *partisan nanoinfluencers*—regular human social media users paid to share political content with less than ten thousand followers—may be chosen because they already ascribe to a particular politics, but many of them are hired simply because of the geographic region they live in, the demographic group they are a part of, or the communities they engage with. Their behavior is like a political form of native advertising on social media. Political groups use these accounts to sow biased information about given issues, candidates, and events—rather than about products or companies.

Sockpuppets and partisan nanoinfluencers are both forms of computational propaganda that use technological tools and platforms to spread coercive political messaging in two ways. Like bots, they explicitly seek to game the curatorial decisions of computational systems, manipulating the algorithms that drive social media engagement to get as many eyes as possible on the propagandistic content. But these types of accounts also operate in another way: they manipulate interpersonal information flows, delivering deceptive or biased material directly to their followers.

The Application of Computational Propaganda

Since at least 2010, a wide variety of political groups have used social media and other online communication tools to spread manipulative partisan messaging.[27] The Tea Party, a populist and antitax conservative group based in the United States, launched one of the earliest known campaigns from the safety of their computers in Iowa.[28] They used automated social media accounts—social bots—on Twitter to spread rumors that Massachusetts's Democratic candidate for Senate, former state attorney general Martha Coakley, was anti-Catholic.[29] Coakley ended up losing the contest to Scott Brown.

In 2018, an eerily similar campaign was pursued against Senator Claire McCaskill, who was running for reelection in a closely contested race in Missouri. The organization CatholicVote "created ad campaigns targeted to mobile devices that have been inside of Catholic churches." They used a variety of messaging tactics to vilify McCaskill, saying she was "pro-abortion . . . , unwilling to protect the Little Sisters of the Poor, and opposed Catholic judicial nominees because of their religious beliefs."[30] The hackers behind these homegrown attacks also worked with the Main Directorate of the General Staff of the Armed Forces of the Russian Federation (known as the GRU) to undermine her campaign online.[31] McCaskill lost.

What changed in the eight years—the better part of a decade—between these two internet-based propaganda campaigns? Nothing and everything. Both propaganda campaigns harnessed social media advertising and varying levels of automation to target specific demographic groups in particular locations with a muddy combination of fact and fancy. Both campaigns used the same digital toolbox, a combination of bots, ads, and memes. And both campaigns went unchecked by the platforms on which the propaganda offensives were partially waged—sites like Facebook and Twitter—and by the politicians in charge of regulating them.

But the tools used, while fundamentally the same, are now exponentially more sophisticated. Today, we deal not with the clunky, fairly obvious bots of the 2010s but with cyborg social media accounts run partly by people, partly by automated computer code—and now we seem to be approaching another evolution in computational propaganda, with sophisticated AI-enabled bots beginning to play a role in the manipulation of political information streams.[32] The propagandists themselves have also changed: they are now much more cunning, battle-hardened after years of working to evade detection and deletion. The strategies for sowing misleading political content have evolved, as has the social context in which this content brews. These propagandists have unprecedented access to specific demographic and personal information from certain platforms, allowing campaigns to more accurately target particular people and subgroups with their propaganda. And as social media has exploded, reaching every corner of the globe, the parameters of the problem have radically expanded, both geographically and in terms of digital reach. We have gone from a few isolated cases occurring over a handful of social media platforms to a global phenomenon that involves media at all levels.[33]

In a little more than a decade, what began as an ad-hoc experiment with using new technology to keep Martha Coakley out of the U.S. Senate—so ad hoc, in fact, that one political strategist described it to me as a digital version of "throw things against the wall and see what sticks"—has now developed into a highly sophisticated and difficult-to-counter political strategy that is helping to decide elections across the globe at all levels of politics.

Why Should We Care About Propaganda in Communication?

The popular dictum about how social media companies make their profit is this: "If you don't know what the product is, the product is you."[34] Facebook, Twitter, and YouTube are for-profit entities focused on making money, but at first glance, it's hard to see what these firms are selling. Events like the 2016 Cambridge Analytica scandal made it clear what they are selling: social media companies store and trade on the vast amounts of personal data we place on their sites and applications. They sell information on our behavior to marketing firms, international conglomerates, and—yes—to political campaigns and their surrogates. Jaron Lanier and others have pushed the idea of users as products a step further. The product is not "you," a single user—the product being sold is imperceptible behavioral change on a massive scale.[35]

Lanier's argument is simple truth, for social media companies make nearly all their income from advertisements, and by definition, the motivation of an advertisement is to *change behavior*. Advertisements try to get someone to buy a product, visit a destination, or support a cause—or to vote a particular way, to support or oppose a particular issue, or even to give up on civic engagement entirely. Uniquely, social media allows not just the familiar, identifiable traditional ads but also native ads—paid content that appears to be authentic, user-generated content. The native ads being run now are often nearly impossible to tell from "organic" content, for regular people can advertise on their own accounts without anyone—the social media firms that run the platforms or their followers—ever knowing they were paid for the content. Much of the time, even Twitter and Facebook don't know what's organic and what's not when it comes from a seemingly real account.

We don't yet really understand the behavioral effects of online ads.[36] It's easy to track whether a given ad on social media gets likes or comments, but it is much harder to track its influence on offline behaviors. This is as true for advertising-driven consumption as it is for online political propaganda. Indeed, it is even more difficult to track the behavioral changes from computational propaganda, which is not overt and identifiable political advertising: it includes the covert political propaganda driven by political bots, sockpuppets, gamed "trending now" social media recommendations, and influencers that I have sketched out above.[37]

What is the measurable effect of these political messages on our actions at the voting booth? Although scholars like Kathleen Hall

Jamieson have argued that it is probable Russian trolls and hackers helped elect Donald Trump in 2016, such academics also rightly point out that there is still a lot we don't know.[38] What is more, we may never have certainty in such situations. But it is still crucial that we gather whatever information we can about how social media alters our lives. A large body of researchers are working to do this. But as Lanier notes, the task is made more difficult by the fact that the behavioral changes caused by online political propaganda are incremental—distributed and sociological in scale, imperceptible at any given moment. Change can happen without being measurable through experimental analyses. Just because we can't easily track a change from point A to point B—trace a line from being exposed to propaganda to voting a certain way—it doesn't mean that change does not happen.

The task is also made more difficult by the fact that, as Ellul pointed out, propaganda is all around us.[39] It's not as easy as tracking a single official campaign advertisement, let alone a comment from a talking head or a Twitter post made by a partisan nanoinfluencer. We simply can't measure these effects at the individual psychological level. Propaganda is inextricable from the whole ecosystem in which we live, with ads, ideas, media technologies, news organizations, and mutable societal norms, values, and beliefs all smashed together. When we attempt to do a controlled experiment—for example, recreate a strand of manipulative political content in a vacuum to try to isolate its effects—it stops being propaganda because it's been separated from the complex sociocultural world in which propaganda operates.

This doesn't mean that we should give up on working to curb politically motivated disinformation or state-sponsored smear campaigns against journalists. What it does mean is that we don't have the luxury of waiting to respond to these problems until we fully understand how they affect human behavior. We must accept that the transmission, or communication, of propaganda leads to all sorts of consequences—some intended, some not—and focus on where the effects are clearest. We can, for instance, work to protect journalists and minority communities—groups that are often the primary targets of computational propaganda campaigns.[40,41,42]

We do know that bots can impact the actions of influential political actors and can change their digital behavior.[43] But to understand political influence in a digital world, we can't focus on tracking pure, empirically evidenced behavioral outcomes—direct notions of change as defined by traditional political science or psychology, which were theorized in an entirely different social and technological world.[44] Instead, we need to think about how to track the diffuse, incremental influence exerted by computational propaganda. Perhaps we should follow the recommendations of scholars like Kate Starbird, focusing on second-order changes rather than first-order ones.[45] In other words, we should focus not on how individual behaviors and ideas change but on how the entire system flexes and evolves. Systemic changes aggregate the changes taking place at the individual level, and they are more easily observed.

Politically motivated groups and individuals continue to regularly use bots in order to boost their communication. We should ask: What does *this* behavior tell us about broader social beliefs and practices? And what does computational propaganda tell us about the new culture of political communication?

The Makers and Trackers of Computational Propaganda

Computational propagandists have two key goals. I've sketched out the first already: to create the illusion of consensus through a bandwagon effect, legitimizing content being spread or manipulated by bots and other tools online and bringing it into parallel, organic conversations by other social media users. The second aims at a rather different version of consensus, one defined by widespread anger, apathy, and polarization—a consensus perhaps more akin to shared discontent. This consensus is designed to make people feel that because everything is terrible, and because the powerful will do what they want regardless, we should just let them do what they want because we can't change things.

The political bot makers I've talked to during this research know that they don't have to actually change people's minds. They simply need the media to regurgitate the algorithmic trends they game or report on the bogus controversies they create. When this happens, ordinary people pick up their intentionally sowed *dis*information— defined by Caroline Jack as "information that is deliberately false or misleading"—and spread it, unwittingly converting the disinformation into *mis*information, or "information whose inaccuracy is unintentional."[46] This is *information laundering*—a kind of relational organizing that takes advantage of people's trust in those they know or feel like they know to legitimize political tall tales and conspiracies.[47] These efforts, many a modern propagandist told me, were enough to sow confusion and polarization or undermine the political process.

The propagandists I interviewed were clear about their intentions and methods. According to someone I'll call Stanley, the head of a conservative U.S. political strategy firm that specializes in digital communication, Donald Trump and his constituents effectively used social media in 2016 as a "megaphone" to prime conversations, on- and offline, about various topics. Stanley openly admitted that he had personal knowledge that U.S. political campaigns were using social media bots to amplify critiques of Hillary Clinton and boost material supporting Trump.[48] The Russian government too used sites like Twitter and Facebook to carry out this kind of manipulation, and propagandists I've interviewed from Istanbul to Quito have made similar claims.

These attempts to manufacture consensus through computational propaganda campaigns are happening worldwide. Some autocratic governments, such as Russia and China, have realized the power of the bot as a tool for waging international cross-border manipulation campaigns; these two governments have used both extant and emerging social media tools in attempts to alter the tenor and flow of information during elections in countries from the Central African Republic to Taiwan to the United States.[49,50] Other autocrats simply seek to build their power at home by manufacturing consensus. For example, Narendra Modi and his Bharatiya Janata Party (BJP) have systematically used automation to spread disinformation over the encrypted messaging platform WhatsApp, seeking to boost their image across the subcontinent while simultaneously harassing and undermining their opposition.[51] Other budding despots around the world—Jair Bolsonaro in Brazil, Rodrigo Duterte in the Philippines, Muhammadu Buhari in Nigeria, and Recep Tayyip Erdoğan in Turkey—have made use of similar automated online tools to amplify their opinions across multiple platforms, from Twitter to YouTube to Facebook.[52,53,54,55] Even nongovernmental groups, ranging from small activist collectives to multinational corporations, are using automated and semi-automated communication technologies to disseminate political content that will benefit them.

Perhaps the scariest computational propagandists, though, are the individual operators who can harness small armies of bogus automated social media accounts and artfully place disinformation for their own means and ends. These are not sophisticated and well-resourced political actor groups like parties, lobbyists, or political consultants; they are simply people with varying motivations and levels of coding skill.[56] These *automated political influencers* may be personal political partisans who are highly invested in the outcome of a particular campaign, or they may be simply mercenaries—paid actors who have little interest in the social context or effects of their work. Whatever their reasons, these automated political influencers are now actors who (like hackers) must be taken seriously by even the most powerful entities.

Updating Understandings of Propaganda: From Broadcast to Digital Media

As the groups who can perpetrate sophisticated digital campaigns have evolved and broadened, so has the nature of the propaganda they produce. The anonymity and automation that are core facets of social media sites like Twitter, YouTube, Reddit, 4chan, and Gab allow propaganda and those who spread it to flourish in new ways. Even Facebook—which has a "real name" policy aimed at allowing only verified users—falls prey to malicious uses of automation, anonymity, and fake accounts on a large scale.[57] Yet these activities do not clearly fit into older definitions of propaganda. It is time for scholars of communication and media to revisit our understanding of propaganda.

In the academy, most theories of propaganda as a communication-based method of control still rely on understandings developed in the era of broadcast media—a time when television, radio, newspapers, and film were the primary media tools and therefore the main vehicles for propaganda. Similarly, those in journalism, government, and the corporate sector who are concerned with propaganda focus on the threat through the lens of past offensives on (or via) these legacy media tools. Today's propaganda is not a top-down, elite-only system of communicative control with relatively clear means and ends; it is a many-to-many mélange of networked, often automated political deceit that originates across a range of online social media applications, quickly spreads to other digital spaces, then makes the jump to legacy media platforms.

Because we are still relying on antiquated notions of propaganda, we struggle to deal with the threat of digital disinformation and other forms of online politicking. We continue to try to use outmoded methods of fact-checking and media literacy, which in our era of virality and "fake news" do not even make a dent. We focus on the activities of political parties and militaries, ignoring that social bots and the networked power of the web now allow nearly *anyone* to spread loaded political messages on a grand scale. We see propaganda as discrete rather than ubiquitous and continuous. In a networked, distributed digital world, modern propaganda cannot be rooted out entirely; we must learn instead to detect it, manage it, and design media and technology systems so that they are not so vulnerable to it.

Traditional social science studies of behavioral influence have long been the gold standard for politically and financially motivated groups who want to change who talks about what. Some methods of influence still in use today are grounded in century-old social science thinking; as Yochai Benkler and colleagues write, "Walter Lippmann's words in *Public Opinion* might as well have been written in 2017 about behavioral psychology, A/B testing, and microtargeting as it was in 1922."[58] But how have these methods evolved with today's media tools? We must update traditional work on propaganda to take account of what we know about contemporary computational propaganda. Only then can we effectively combat attempts to manufacture consensus. Understanding digital propaganda in the context of long-held ideas about human belief and action can also properly contextualize our societal concerns about these problems, for propaganda has existed for as long as humans have leveraged media to influence opinion. It has always been both technological and social.

Yes, it has been bolstered by media-based innovations throughout the ages and has evolved to take advantage of each shift, but this is not necessarily cause for doomsaying. We don't know the societal outcomes of computational propaganda yet, and broadcast media's hysteria about it may be more effective at causing polarization or political apathy than political bots could ever be.

Policymakers and social media companies continue to struggle to make sense of, and control, this new computational propaganda. During the 2020 U.S. presidential election, the U.S. government failed to deal with the use of social media bots and other inorganic information manipulation tactics such as partisan nanoinfluence. Firms like Facebook and their subsidiary WhatsApp are simply treading water in the face of what they call "information operations," despite the increasing urgency of the problem: viral misleading and violent content is a real threat in, for example, India and Myanmar, where people have been killed after particularly effective computational propaganda campaigns.[59,60,61]

We need to move toward a more unified understanding of modern propaganda—who does it, what it looks like, when it is most likely to occur, why we consume it, and how it works. We need new theories that will connect the dots among the answers to these questions and contextualize the ongoing empirical work on the subject. The ideas I present in this book, particularly its central notion of "manufacturing consensus," are a step toward bringing our concept of propaganda into the present day.

Methods

This work is part of an established tradition of scholarly efforts that study people and technology using qualitative techniques. This ethnographic or field-based research allows me to systematically describe the norms, values, and beliefs of both propagandists and their targets. It helps me to paint a picture, through the descriptions and stories in the following chapters, of the people behind the tools. Who are they? Why do they do what they do? How do they do it? What digital tools are central to their efforts?

The findings in this book are drawn from a variety of different sorts of fieldwork: networked (spread over multiple locations or field sites); information oriented (online ethnographic work); and of course traditional, face-to-face ethnographic study. I see this project as complementing big-data analyses of information from social media. That work illuminates quantitative details about political bots and their networks and communication; this project focuses on the qualities of political bot usage, as I try to understand what makers and trackers of computational propaganda feel about their activities, particularly as they relate to political contests and other civic events, and investigate their broader views about the flow of information over social media and emerging digital media tools.

What follows is an account of my eight years of international field research with the people who build and use bots to spread and track propaganda or to fight it. The concept of *manufacturing consensus* that I put forward here is drawn from interviews with over one hundred people around the world who have allegiances to numerous varying political groups and professions. Four distinct actor groups are at the center of this book: (1) political campaign workers, (2) technology industry experts, (3) journalists, and (4) automated political influencers. During my years of research, I spoke to people on all sides of the issue: people actively building and launching computational propaganda campaigns, tech industry experts and journalists working to respond to the growing threat of disinformation and online manipulation, and people who were on the receiving end of propaganda. All of their stories are here, and they provide the foundation for the solutions that I propose throughout.

My interviews with global experts focused on making and tracking computational propaganda provide particular insight into how these communicative technologies played a part during pivotal political events from North America to the Middle East. I most regularly refer to the propagandistic use of bots over social media during political events in four countries: Ecuador, the United States, the United Kingdom, and Turkey. In order to provide background and contextual information, I also discuss cases of computational propaganda in a number of other countries around the globe: Brazil, Germany, Hungary, India, Japan, Mexico, Russia, the Philippines, South Korea, Taiwan, and Ukraine.

In order to understand where and with whom computational propaganda was originating, I spent time in several of the above countries during elections and other political events. I attended campaign gatherings, sat in on digital strategy workshops, visited major news outlets, went to conferences, and collaborated with social media companies and other technology firms. I wanted to develop a broad sense of the culture of the people spreading and tracking computational propaganda. Observation formed a portion of this work—I was regularly shown examples of bots and sockpuppet accounts in the wild. In order to gain access to those in the know about digital political strategy and actual political bot use, I had to spend time learning the ins and outs of the technology at hand. I had to scour the web and leverage connections (using a snowball sampling technique, discussed in more detail below) in order to meet the right people and learn the structures of various actor groups. I even learned to build simple bots; for the 2018 exhibit *The Future Starts Here* at London's Victoria and Albert Museum, I worked with a colleague to build an interactive political bot on Twitter aimed at educating people about computational propaganda.

It was difficult to get bot makers and propagandists to speak to me, let alone to divulge information on their illicit political communication activities. Illicit bot makers do careful work to stay hidden, and many of their campaigns are designed to be anonymous, deliberately hiding their origins. I was lucky to have colleagues who had conducted global qualitative work on digital political activism and control. They were able to put me in touch with a variety of people and political groups in North America, Europe, North Africa, and the Middle East with whom they had established connections. These contacts connected me with early-stage interviewees in these regions, who in turn grew into contacts elsewhere around the world.

This is called snowball sampling: you start with a few contacts who start the ball rolling, and they introduce you to others, who introduce you to still others. This technique is often used by researchers who work with hard to reach or potentially hostile interview subjects, and it was a core method for my own work among political bot builders and propagandists. Once introduced to a potential interviewee with expertise on the latest propaganda techniques, I would often exchange numerous encrypted e-mails or private messages (using Signal or Telegram) with them, describing my project. I would estimate that one in every ten or fifteen e-mails resulted in a response, and perhaps one in thirty resulted in an interview. Surprisingly, though, once someone committed to being interviewed—after having gone through extensive back-and-forth on my project and having read and verbally consented to the informed consent document—they were quite candid about their influence-oriented activities. This was likely due, at least in part, to the fact that I spoke with all interview subjects on the condition of anonymity. This was a considered choice, oriented toward making them as safe and comfortable as possible. Other interviewees seemed willing to participate because they did not see anything wrong with their actions; these people either felt distanced from the work because they were paid to do it or they were proud of it, seeing it as innovative and clever.

In order to stay up to date and locate other potential interview subjects, I signed up for every mailer I could find on social bots, social media politics, and propaganda. I followed key players (and hundreds of bots) on social media and religiously went through their public messages and metadata. Political bot and sockpuppet accounts are often short-lived. Either they fulfill their task and are then taken down by their deployers to avoid a trail, or they are deleted by social media platforms because they violate terms of service, showing signs of spam or being used to harass other users. I regularly catalogued screenshots of known political bots and sockpuppets in order to save examples of particular tactics and types and to preserve now non-existent (beyond the odd Wayback Machine snapshot) automated accounts. I made notations about what accounts showed signs of high automation; these notes, as well as my screenshots and other field notes, were stored using Zotero and Microsoft Excel. These notes were stored securely in an encrypted hard drive in a place separate from my computer.

I followed relevant events and important moments online when I could not be there in person, using news reports, community documents, and archived social media material to understand what happened. I also gathered secondhand accounts of these events via one-on-one interviews with experts who had been in attendance or who had worked on particular computational propaganda campaigns. I often heard contradictions in stories of how events played out, or in how automation or other social media tools were used. Political campaigns, journalists, and activists regularly disagreed about how things happened—about what truth looked like. To get to the bottom of discrepancies in accounts, I worked to triangulate the competing accounts with online narratives from multiple sources.

Chapter Outline

In the following pages, I use the propaganda theories of the past to explain the gaps in our knowledge today and show how updating those foundational theories can help us better understand today's media landscape. I explain how the media through which we receive propaganda have changed and demonstrate that technologies like bots, alongside recommendation algorithms and advances in artificial intelligence (AI), have changed both the scale and scope of propaganda. I show how two particular features of social media, automation and anonymity, are central to the practice of computational propaganda. I discuss the changing face of the propagandist, suggesting that we take into consideration new actor groups active in the spread of political spin, particularly the automated political influencer. In outlining this emerging group, I discuss the ways the production of propaganda, like the production of information writ large, has become democratized: as I show, anyone can now build and launch political manipulation campaigns online.

Chapter 2 reviews how propaganda has been understood in times past. I build on, amend, and alter existing theories of propaganda to take account of the current era. This new theoretical work extends the propaganda model of Herman and Chomsky and complicates their view of the machinations of the mass media. I leverage their perspective, which is grounded in political economy, alongside the work of current media theorists and science and technology studies (STS) scholars in order to focus on the problems posed by propaganda in the era of the internet, particularly as they relate to communication, journalism, and media studies.

In chapters 3–6, I share evidence, stories, and insights from my years of fieldwork with the people who produce and track computational propaganda: those who spread this automated, social media–borne political manipulation and those who track and report on it. I describe my discussions with political campaign workers, technology industry experts, journalists, and automated political influencers, uncovering how they feel about the political use of bots, sockpuppets, partisan nanoinfluencers—why and how they do what they do. The chapters alternate between the perspectives of interviewees from well-resourced and well-organized groups: governments and social media corporations are discussed in chapters 3 and 5, and automated political influencers and journalists—those from less-resourced and less-organized groups—are discussed in chapters 4 and 6.

In chapter 3, I describe the activities of state-based producers of computational propaganda. Much of the early research into the political use of bots and social media focused on governmental use, which is the basis of traditional top-down models of propaganda. As I show, governments are still the most well-resourced—and therefore perhaps the most effective—users of computational propaganda. In this chapter, I discuss how political elites work to manufacture consensus using what I call "state-sponsored trolling."[62] I also show that some governments, particularly Russia and India, have rapidly adapted old propaganda strategies to new digital tools, while others, such as the United States and United Kingdom, are still adjusting to the new informational landscape.

In chapter 4, I consider how ordinary people—usually individuals, often with little to no financial backing and sometimes even with little technological know-how—use political bots and other tools and strategies. I call this unique and amorphous actor group "automated political influencers": *automated* because they rely on bots in some way to spread their messaging; *political* because the messages they spread are concerned with political events, ideas, and people; and *influencers* because they market their ideas on social media. The core transportable idea of this chapter is the concept of *democratized propaganda*—the internet and social media–enabled use of political manipulation by the masses. This concept emerged years into my work on computational propaganda; it took so long because I was hung up on the digital activities of powerful political entities. Through my fieldwork, though, I realized that many of the producers and trackers of bot-centric propaganda did not work for governments, political parties, militaries, or intelligence services. Many worked in loose collectives or individually, motivated by political beliefs or money (or both). Here, I show that while automated political influencers are less organized and less resourced than governments, they are able to efficiently leverage guerilla marketing strategies to break through to virality and "mainstream" media coverage, and sometimes they get picked up by governments and made part of larger organizations.

In chapter 5, I zoom back out to examine the technology industry's role in facilitating computational propaganda and manufactured consensus. This chapter returns to lessons learned from Herman and Chomsky about big media's role in spreading propaganda. Here, though, the "big media" is big *social* media: new, globally powerful firms like Google and Facebook, which are deeply complicit in political manipulation campaigns across their various social media products. Contemporary versions of the traditional mass media of Herman and Chomsky's day (such as major media firms like Disney and News Corp) still play a large role in fostering propaganda, but they rarely do so by directly producing new propagandistic content. Instead, they spread propaganda by reacting to manipulative content on social media. In this chapter, I focus on the notion of bot-based algorithmic manipulation, sharing stories from interviewees which show that often their primary intentions were to use large numbers of bots to trick social media sites' trending algorithms; they wanted Facebook, YouTube, and Twitter to push propagandistic content on their front pages or sidebars, hoping that the content would be picked up by traditional news media. As I show, social media firms have known that this type of algorithmic gaming was a systemic problem, but they have failed to respond to it quickly or comprehensively enough.

In chapter 6, I zero in on journalism, exploring how reporters and news organizations are responding to the problem of computational propaganda. I show that some journalists seek to fight fire with fire, using social and political bots in their own work to keep up with the reach and volume of automated propaganda. Journalists often use bots as what I call *information radiators*, a term that came up in my interview with Al, a journalist who also built and used social media bots. I show how journalism (usually unwittingly) is exacerbating the problem: journalists often unintentionally amplify and legitimize disinformation spread by computational propaganda.[63] This is, in part, a structural problem, for news organizations are extremely underresourced—largely because social media companies have usurped their reporting and the advertising that had provided revenue for news sources.[64] Journalists are also frequently the primary targets of computational propaganda attacks and large-scale online trolling campaigns. Political bots are used to stop journalists from communicating about particular stories or ideas due to fear of isolation and reprisal.[65]

The conclusion offers up a summary of the core arguments of this book and discusses paths for future research on political bots and the people who build and track them. I consider ways in which computational propaganda is changing—how both bots and their masters are becoming more sophisticated. Now, organized groups of human users (partisan nanoinfluencers) are making it more difficult than ever to detect manufactured consensus and bogus social media trends. I outline new incarnations of propaganda, most notably geo-propaganda and encrypted propaganda, which rely on geolocation tools and closed messaging apps, respectively. Finally, I offer up some solutions to computational propaganda—pragmatic ideas on how to respond to the problem, aimed at policymakers, academics, technologists, and others.

2

Understanding Manufactured Consensus

Democracy has proclaimed the dictatorship of palaver, and the technique of dictating to the dictator is propaganda.

Harold D. Lasswell [1]

Introduction

In Narendra Modi's India, propaganda has quickly become a way of life. Under the rule of the Bharatiya Janata Party (BJP; in English, the Indian People's Party), India's citizens are now subject to a chaotic torrent of misinformation, disinformation, and junk news. In India, the social media app of choice is WhatsApp, the closed messaging service owned by Facebook. On WhatsApp, people can communicate directly with individual friends or family members or chat with groups of up to 256 people. In these WhatsApp groups, Modi's "information yoddhas" (warriors, in Hindi) work tirelessly to seed and fertilize biased and deceptive political content that users then spread across their communities. This misinformation has had real offline consequences: particular strands of misinformation on WhatsApp—including offensives tied to the BJP—have led to mob violence, including rape and murder. [2]

Since September 2019, my research team at the University of Texas has been working to understand the flow of propaganda on encrypted messaging apps (EMAs) like WhatsApp. We've spoken to several people—some affiliated with the BJP and some not—that either took part in running propaganda over EMAs in India or have special expertise on the subject. What we've learned from these conversations, and from our broader research on the subject, has revealed a computational propaganda framework of enormous reach and power. Not only do BJP "IT cells" use political bots to spread content on WhatsApp, they mobilize both small and large groups of people to sow propaganda and actively respond to critiques of Modi and his government. Their focus is regional, and those we interviewed claim that there are thousands of such cells or groups across the country, each geared toward spreading a combination of national news cultivated in the BJP offices in New Delhi and regional news created in situ.

Interviewees, some of whom maintain other day jobs while they oversee BJP EMA propaganda operations, describe IT cells with multiple employees, hundreds of Android phones, and various forms of amplification technology. Some brag about using people rather than political bots in order to evade WhatsApp's detection mechanisms; others openly use political bots and claim great success at having their inorganic political content picked up and spread organically by other social media users. According to these people, the particular power of WhatsApp is that it is intimate: people mostly engage with those whom they know. There are certainly cracks—WhatsApp is not limited to intimate, personal connections, and sometimes small groups are invaded by strangers spreading disinformation from the BJP for pay. But many times, friends and family members spread misinformation seen elsewhere (including elsewhere on WhatsApp) because it fits with their own beliefs. By and large, the BJP understands WhatsApp as a powerful tool for relational advertising.[3] As my colleague Jacob puts it, they know that you might not trust a mainstream media source, but you trust your grandma. The detection and deletion efforts of WhatsApp and its parent company, Facebook, fall short when the harmful propaganda and disinformation is being spread by real people. And WhatsApp is a particularly difficult platform to police because it uses what is known as end-to-end encryption—meaning that information can be read only by the sender and receiver of messages, and only once it is decrypted.

The propagandistic messaging spread over WhatsApp is, as you might expect, highly varied in terms of both its partisan perspective and its informational quality. There is content lauding Modi and the BJP, and there is content demonizing them. There are messages, voice notes, and videos that attack the BJP's opposition, and there are similar communications that support other parties. There is misinformation and disinformation, but there is also quality news and genuine political debate. The genius of the BJP's WhatsApp information operations—and computational propaganda campaigns more broadly—is not necessarily that they produce blind support for a nationalist, right-wing agenda. It is the BJP's understanding that intimate messages among friends make disinformation more potent, and that a closed communication system is exploitable in ways that are not possible on open platforms like YouTube, Facebook, or Twitter. This same principle has led to metastatic encrypted disinformation around the globe in countries like Brazil, Mexico, and Taiwan.

In our interviews with BJP operatives and experts, it has become clear that the WhatsApp-centric informational system is fairly messy and segmented, as are the attempts to spread propaganda using it. But our interviewees don't seem to mind this relative chaos. In fact, this seems to complement their intentions. They can exert a kind of control over the media system by promoting disarray within it—disarray that, given the networked nature of the digital media landscape, often flows back to traditional media outlets. On WhatsApp, myriad political groups and interests, armed mostly with smartphones, use a highly automated and anonymous media tool in an effort to get their voices—and their propaganda—heard. They have learned to manipulate the legitimate media to amplify their message.

From Broadcast Propaganda
to Computational Propaganda

This chapter gives a brief historical overview of scholarly conceptualizations of propaganda, summarizing the core arguments of scholars including Walter Lippmann, Harold D. Lasswell, Edward L. Bernays, Jacques Ellul, Edward S. Herman and Noam Chomsky, Garth S. Jowett and Victoria J. O'Donnell, Stanley B. Cunningham, and others.[4,5,6,7,8,9,10] I identify the gaps in these traditional definitions and discuss how the propaganda model presented by Herman and Chomsky can be expanded for the era of digital media. Finally, I offer a brief exemplar of how modern computational propaganda works as a chaotic, many-to-many means of manipulating public opinion: the 2016 U.S. election.

The way we see propaganda today is deeply rooted in theories created by early scholars of communication and media. Their work, much of it from the early twentieth century, was instrumental in developing, institutionalizing, and legitimizing what we now know as social science—the study of human behavior, society, and relationships. The early research into propaganda, focused as it was on how people exerted control over others using various media tools, grew out of trailblazing inquiry in fields from sociology to psychology, economics to political science, media studies to communication.[11] The cross-disciplinary nature of propaganda as a field of study reveals a larger truth about this mutating topic: as a problem, it permeates every aspect of society. The issue of propaganda is both social and technical. It is social in that propaganda, created by people for a wide variety of reasons, has unexpected and far-reaching consequences on society once released.[12] It is technical because technology allows propaganda to scale in sheer volume and potency. The dual social/ technical nature of propaganda has never been more clear than it is today. Social media systems provide a tremendously fertile playing field that offers access to many, many citizens at all levels of society, and technical tools such as political bots and sockpuppets extend the reach and volume of propaganda.

As with any communication phenomenon, propaganda can be analyzed beginning from three angles: its *reception*, its *content*, and its *production*. Different fields of study examine propaganda differently, and any given discipline can study propaganda by way of any of these three angles. Psychological research, an early field of work on propaganda, has focused largely on reception, asking why people consume propaganda and what makes them susceptible to it. Reception is the focus of political scientists such as Harold Lasswell, who also examines content, analyzing the rhetorical power of propaganda. Political economists have generally focused on production—on how and why governments or other powerful actors use propaganda to enforce their political will on the populace. Sociologists, anthropologists, and scholars of communication and media have historically taken a broader view, looking at propaganda as a sociocultural phenomenon that should be measured via reception and deeply explored via ethnographic research on all three angles—production, content, and reception.

In this book, I focus primarily on the production of propaganda but from a communication, media studies, and ethnographically informed perspective. By analyzing the people who make novel forms of propaganda using new media tools, I hope to build our understanding of contemporary propagandists' goals and their relationships to power. What can historical research on propaganda, particularly that produced alongside the advent of radio and its successive broadcast modes of communication, reveal about the production of propaganda today? How has propaganda stayed the same, and how has it evolved?

Before the twentieth century, *propaganda* was not a dirty word used to describe illicit political manipulation but simply a term for describing a means of "enlightened rule."[13] The word itself emerged in 1622, derived from the Vatican's Office for the Propagation of Faith, which worked to "supervise the Church's missionary efforts in the New World and elsewhere." This earliest propaganda was intended to spread not lies but truth: "Far from denoting lies, half-truths, selective history or any of the other tricks that we associate with propaganda now, that word meant, at first, the total opposite of such deceptions."[14] The church saw it as a tool for *preventing* deception by bringing people into the faith (though I'm sure the people on the receiving end of their ministrations saw it quite differently). With industrialization, the definition of propaganda morphed somewhat away from its Catholic roots, though the concept still largely held a positive valence. As new media forms (particularly the modern newspaper) emerged with the Industrial Revolution, governments and other power groups gained new ways of reaching the populace. The notion of propaganda was still tied to a form of evangelism—this time political rather than religious.[15] Mass media was beginning to usher in a more heavy-handed politics of spin.

After the First World War, a growing body of work on contemporary propaganda viewed it as a qualified good—a tool for using the growing broadcast media system to ensure smooth governance of the masses and support the functioning of democracy.[16] It is easy today to overlook this fact: many early scholars of broadcast-era propaganda *supported* it as a tool for "the engineering of consent" among the masses.[17,18] The context in which this position emerged is important. Lippmann, Bernays, and Lasswell were writing in the aftermath of World War I, at a time when the democratic fervor that had accompanied the conflict was languishing and regime changes, revolutions, and uprisings were popping up across Eastern Europe, Russia, and the Middle East. Their perspectives on propaganda as a means of "managing collective attitudes" using new broadcast technology were thus more utilitarian than moralistic.

However, Bernays and the other pragmatic propaganda apologists eventually lost the battle to frame governmental propaganda as a necessary democratic tool. After World War I, the general populace in the United States and Western Europe were exceptionally wary of propaganda—both the term and the practice. Most people in the United States realized they had been thoroughly manipulated by homegrown propaganda after the war, when a great deal of revelatory writing came out on the subject. People didn't like that they had been maneuvered, no matter the reasons behind the manipulation. Lasswell's 1926 PhD dissertation, "Propaganda Technique in the World War," provided a thorough, if sometimes antiwar-oriented, discussion of information manipulation campaigns during the event—analytically parsing efforts from both the Allied and Central Powers.[19] With the emerging dominance of the Nazi Party in Germany, and later throughout Europe, many academics, journalists, and psychologists were pulled into German propaganda efforts. Correspondingly, similar individuals were pulled together by the Allied forces in counterefforts. Again, as in World War I, propaganda emerged as a given information control practice undertaken by all sides.

By the 1960s, scholarly investigations of propaganda were shifting toward examining the phenomenon within its social and historical contexts. Propaganda was no longer seen as a simple conveyance of information, delivered via a one-to-one or one-to-many channel by a specific figure (like Bernays's "public relations counsel"). Instead,

Jacques Ellul, the central figure in this scholarly shift, argued that propaganda is a sociological phenomenon—a multifaceted, situational, and unpredictable force that is crucially propelled by technology.[20] For Ellul (and for me), propaganda is "the Siamese twin of our technological society": it is intrinsically tied to (and increases people's reliance on) the myriad technologies entering society in the aftermath of World War II, particularly television, film, and radio.[21] Ellul argued that all angles of human life were being "technicized," and that this had allowed for the deluge of propaganda. As he saw it, people were becoming slaves to their technology, and propaganda was the communicative and sociological means of this enslavement. Ellul's focus on the technological means of producing and disseminating propaganda informs my approach in this book.

By the time Herman and Chomsky wrote the first edition of *Manufacturing Consent* in 1988, the social sciences had largely moved away from the study of propaganda. Their research amended and extended the social science work of Lippmann, Lasswell, Bernays, and Ellul, shifting away from more purely psychological or sociological concerns and toward notions of power and the means of production. For them, propaganda was a political-economic phenomenon in which extremely powerful mass media entities acted as mouthpieces for the elite actors who funded them. This top-down view of propaganda, threaded through with some strands of thought retained from the original post–World War I scholarship of propaganda, remains the foundation of today's scholarship of propaganda, which is largely concerned with the communicative machinations of nation-states, corporations, and other powerful actors, and particularly the role played by government-friendly (and sometimes, as with RT and Sputnik, state-owned) media entities like Fox News and Breitbart in the United States, Televisa in Mexico and throughout the Spanish-speaking world, RT and Sputnik in Russia, and the Central European Press and Media Foundation in Hungary.[22,23,24,25]

The variety of different strains of propaganda research, and the differing conceptions of propaganda that they have produced, mean that there is no clear-cut, agreed-upon picture of what propaganda is, what it does, how it does it, and to whom. Is it something enacted by actors upon a populace? Is it a sociotechnical phenomenon? Or is it indoctrination by way of a subservient mass media? According to Benkler and colleagues, we must keep in mind propaganda's definitional aim of changing public opinion and behavior: "In appropriating the term 'propaganda' to describe the broad structure of ideology in modern, technologically mediated society, as Ellul did, or the failings of the commercial media during the rise of neoliberalism, as Herman and Chomsky did, the critical turn removed the term 'propaganda' from the toolkit of those who wish to study intentional manipulation of public opinion, particularly as it applied to publics." These authors suggest that it is most useful to "revive the technocratic or scientific study of propaganda as a coherent topic of analysis."[26] This work has been carried out by scholars such as Jowett and O'Donnell, who seek to systematically historicize and define propaganda and to develop an analytical approach to studying it.[27] While there is much of value in their work and that of Benkler and colleagues, these scholars are inclined toward picking back up the positivist approach to the study of propaganda that was common in Lippmann's time. Because of this, they fail to take into account the problems, enumerated in chapter 1, with attempting to study propaganda's effects via a positivist or post-positivist lens.

My research draws on much of this previous scholarship, synthesizing and extending it. After spending years talking to the people who make and track bot-borne propaganda, as well as those who construct other novel and technologically enhanced strands of manipulation via media, I'm inclined to view today's propaganda via the combined insights offered by Lippmann, Bernays, Ellul, and Herman and Chomsky. In particular, I believe that Chomsky and Herman's work, which adapts prior research on propaganda to the era of mass media, is highly useful and relevant to our current situation. Ellul's scholarship, too, is especially central to this book, particularly his core argument about the pitfalls of treating propaganda as a static phenomenon whose effects can only be determined experimentally, in isolation: "[Many scholars] establish a certain image or definition of propaganda, and proceed to the study of whatever corresponds to their definition; or yielding to the attraction of scientific study, they try to experiment with some particular method of propaganda on small groups and in small doses—at which moment it ceases to be propaganda."[28]

Like Ellul, I believe that in order "to study propaganda we must turn not to the psychologist, but to the propagandist."[29] Propaganda is something that occurs *in situ*, at the site of application and with particular goals in mind—but also alongside and in between all manner of other intentions, messages, and understandings. It is a messy combination of particular people attempting to control others, sociotechnical forces, and mass-mediated indoctrination—and the introduction of the web and social media have made it even messier. With the potent combination of propagandists preying on the opinions of the masses, of sociological and technical forces, of controlled mass media, and of novel digital media tools, we are at a conjunction where the information ecosystem is flooded by a complex, cross-amplifying, global mixture of multifaceted propaganda. The propaganda landscape we face now is the culmination of Lippmann's, Ellul's, and Herman and Chomsky's notions of propaganda, with a novel digital twist.

In the following section, I take a deeper dive into the work of these scholars, with a primary focus on the propaganda model of Herman and Chomsky. I explain how the use of digital tools—particularly of automation and algorithms—changes the nature of propaganda. I provide an updated version of Herman and Chomsky's model that takes account of these new tools. I also show how technological features such as automation and anonymity, and the social shift past the Western fear of communism and into a broader fear of the other side (whoever that may be), have fundamentally altered the use of propaganda today.

From Lippmann and Bernays to Ellul to Herman and Chomsky

As I note in the first chapter, Herman and Chomsky popularized the phrase "manufacturing consent," which they used to describe the task of indoctrination carried out by broadcast media giants controlled by particular financial and political interests. However, the phrase did not originate with them; they borrowed and retooled it from the work of Walter Lippmann (and his follower Edward Bernays), who spoke of "the manufacture of consent."[30] Lippmann saw the potential of technology to extend and intensify the effects of propaganda, writing "that the manufacture of consent is capable of great refinements no one, I think, denies." However, he saw propaganda as a necessary evil that enabled democracy to succeed. For him, there could be no perfect rule by the people. Rather, an enlightened few—including journalists and media makers—were to leverage propaganda in order to mold public opinion into a shape that allowed for continued liberty and equality via rational rule.[31] Lippmann, who was disenchanted with socialism, drew on the work of John Dewey,

Graham Wallas, William James, Gustave Le Bon, and George Santayana to theorize that "fictions determine[d] a very great part of [peoples'] political behavior."[32] Because most voters were uncritical and self-deluding, he argued, they had to be controlled through the somewhat subjective crafting of fact. The pragmatic Lippmann framed the manipulation of public opinion as being simply "the effort to alter the picture to which men respond, to substitute one social pattern for another."[33] He believed that experts, who had a better grasp of "facts," would make the proper social pattern intelligible for the masses—a form of propaganda.

Bernays was greatly inspired by Lippmann's work. True, Bernays referred to the "engineering" of consent rather than the manufacturing of it, but his central idea was still the same: the strategy of mass persuasion for purposes of control.[34] For Bernays, the control was being sought by forces both corporate and political, and those controlling the narrative were not, for him, journalists or thinkers but what he called a "public relations counsel," an advertiser or marketer of ideas. In the years following World War I, Bernays, the "farsighted architect of modern propaganda," leveraged understandings of psychology—including theories on subconscious desire pioneered by his uncle Sigmund Freud—to carry out manipulation campaigns on behalf of big business and government.[35] For Bernays, PR and propaganda were two faces of the same technique—manipulating opinion to refine and retain power for the corporate and political realms, which he saw as inextricably connected. Bernays believed in promoting propaganda via "established mediums of communication," such as newspapers, magazines, and movies, as well as influential figures who already had the ear of the public.[36] Like Lippmann, Bernays believed that "the conscious and intelligent manipulation of the organized habits and opinions of the masses is an important element in democratic society," but the ends he put it to were less lofty.[37]

Jacques Ellul's perspective about the use of propaganda was both less utilitarian and less controlled than the views of Lippmann and Bernays. For Ellul, propaganda was not simply targeted communication for a particular manipulative purpose but pervasive and sociological, a "very general phenomenon," and no one person could entirely avoid its reach. He argued that propaganda is "made . . . because of a will to action for the purpose of effectively arming policy and giving irresistible power to its decisions." It occurs across all governance types and is not dependent on the state or entity that originally perpetuated it. According to Ellul, propaganda is not simply evil, a set of "tall stories"; it is a whole sociotechnical way of doing things, one that promotes technical progress and helps to entrench a technologically centric world. It is "the means used to prevent [increasing mechanization and technological organization] from being felt as too oppressive and to persuade [people] to submit with good grace."[38]

So how did Herman and Chomsky synthesize these two distinct but related views of propaganda? The world of Lippmann and Bernays framed propaganda as a task for the elite—the journalist, the politician, and the businessperson (or the public relations counsel acting on their behalf)—who sought to deliver tailored "facts" to the masses for the sake of democracy. Bernays, in particular, tied the corporate and the political together, presenting propaganda as a pragmatic means for the elite few to present their messages to the many. Ellul picked up their notion of propaganda as a planned, intentional mechanism of control, but he more thoroughly factored in its societal diffuseness and its technological means and ends. Herman and Chomsky borrowed something from each of these philosophies: Lippmann and Bernays's view of propaganda as something done by one group (the mass media and its elite shepherds) to another (the people) and Ellul's view of propaganda as something achieved by way of advanced technological and social systems. Herman and Chomsky's model of propaganda adds to these, taking into account both the goals of the powerful and the rise of broadcast technology and the tuned-in society it produced to create a concise argument about the inner workings of propaganda in the 1980s (and, in their later edition, the 1990s).

Based on case studies on the U.S. media's handling of a number of crises, Herman and Chomsky believed that the media "propagandize[d] on behalf of" those who "controlled and financed them."[39] Crucially, though, they were primarily interested in the *production* of propaganda, not on its reception; they were not interested in how well it worked, only why and by whom it was created. According to them, their model "describe[s] forces that shape what the media does; it does not imply that any propaganda emanating from the media are successful."[40] Herman and Chomsky's "analytical framework" thus focused on explaining the communicative function of U.S. media in relation to institutional structure and the societal interests that control it. I pick up this perception of media's role in the propaganda cycle later, discussing a similar role among major social media firms.

In the 2002 update of their original work, Herman and Chomsky take account of the further consolidation of media ownership since their original edition. They also nod to the potential political effects of the internet, noting that "some argue the internet and the new communications technologies are breaking the corporate stranglehold on journalism and opening up an unprecedented era of interactive democratic media." They acknowledge the ways in which the web has opened up social networking and political activism, but by and large they see the commercialization of the internet—of both the hardware and software that constitute it—as "threaten[ing] to limit any future prospects of the internet as a democratic media vehicle."[41] How right they are. This is the line of reasoning that I pick up in my amendment of their propaganda model for the digital age. Herman and Chomsky wrote their second edition in a time *just* before the explosion of social media. As sites like Facebook were coming into prominence, scholars were still arguing for the democratizing potential of the internet and discussing the liberating merits of social media.[42] But very soon it became clear that social media combined corporate control of online social spaces with an increasing normalization of online political manipulation, and that it could no longer to be read as primarily a tool of liberation.[43]

Amending Herman and Chomsky for the Digital Age

I began studying computational propaganda in hopes of understanding how communication on social media was being controlled, looking for online spaces left for democratic organization. I still believe that social media and liberation need not be mutually exclusive: one need look no further than the Hong Kong protests in 2019 to see how both old and new social media sites play a role in the communication efforts of grassroots democracy groups. The U.S. uprisings surrounding the murder of George Floyd and the Thai and Belarusian protests in 2020 reveal the same uses. But I found that computational propaganda, like other types of propaganda through history, is grounded in seemingly intractable structures of power. It is governed by a complex interplay between commercial and political interests—between companies and political groups with a stake in both online and offline communication and media. I also found that certain features of digital communication—specifically, anonymity and automation—make computational propaganda more insidious and dangerous than previous forms of print, radio, and television propaganda.

To explain modern propaganda, Chomsky and Herman's model must be updated to account for social media and computational propaganda. Their original conceptual model is made up of five "filters" that operate as constituent parts central to the functioning of propaganda via the U.S. mass media: (1) size, ownership, and profit orientation of the mass media; (2) the advertising license to do business; (3) sourcing mass media news; (4) flak and the enforcers; and (5) anticommunism as a control mechanism. In what follows, I update these five filters for the digital age.

Herman and Chomsky's first filter—the size, ownership, and profit orientation of the media—pertains to the rise of media conglomerates that are guided by the capitalist imperative to make money and satisfy shareholders above all else. According to Herman and Chomsky, this orientation sets the mass media up as mouthpieces for the powerful rather than as champions for common people. They outline the nineteenth-century rise of the radical press among the working class in the United Kingdom. This media "of the people" was designed to create a common cause for workers and offered an "alternative value system and framework for looking at the world."[44] Unsurprisingly, this people's press and the working-class unification it promoted were seen as a major problem by those in power. Eventually, elites were able to use the "free" market to strangle and supplant the radical press. As papers grew, so too did financial costs—the press became industrialized and small printers could not compete. The first filter, Herman and Chomsky argue, grew out of this industrialization of the news media.

Their description of the stranglehold of capital on media ("The limitation on ownership of the media with any substantial outreach by the requisite large size of investment") is as true today as it was thirty-odd years ago—and indeed, as it was in the late 1800s.[45] But the problem today is not mass media, as it was in Herman and Chomsky's period of interest. Today, while media companies like AT&T and the Fox Corporation are still powerful brokers of information, it is *new* media firms like Google and Facebook that exert primary control over the flow of information. My amendment to the first filter lies in simply adding digital media providers whose sheer size, consolidated ownership, and profit orientation make them ideal mechanisms of propaganda. Modern examples of this first filter include Google, Facebook, Amazon, Weibo, VK, and Tencent; smaller social media and digital firms like Twitter, Tumblr, ByteDance, Snap, LinkedIn, Hulu, Netflix, and Mail.ru; and hardware-centric tech companies like Apple and Microsoft. As experts have pointed out, these tech and social media companies now exert an immeasurable amount of control over the marketplaces of products and ideas.[46]

The second filter of Herman and Chomsky's propaganda model, the fact that advertising funds most media (which they call the "advertising license to do business"), is similarly relevant to propaganda in the age of social media. They note that advertising, like media consolidation, was a market-oriented nail in the coffin of the radical free press. Indeed, advertising intensified the consolidation of media, for it favored large media companies: "An advertising-based system," they note, "will tend to drive out of existence or into marginality the media companies and types that depend on the revenue of sales alone."[47] This began with newspapers. Newspapers leveraged the money they made via ads to subsidize a copy price that was much lower than production costs demanded, meaning papers that didn't use advertising had to contend with higher prices, dropping sales (in the face of cheaper papers), and less money to invest in making a product that was more appealing. This also holds true with social media today. Most major social media companies primarily rely on advertising (along with the sale of user data) for their profits. Platforms with large advertising revenues can undercut competitors that attempt to use different profit (or nonprofit) models.

Social media firms' use of advertising has crowded out traditional broadcast and print media, who use the same model with less refinement and reach. The takeover of the prime share of the global advertising market by Facebook, Google, and other firms has given them primacy as propaganda actors; their algorithms and trends alter, and even dictate, much of the news that users see—and that legacy media companies report on.[48] These firms and algorithms hold the keys to legacy media companies' access to digital consumers: their ability to successfully reach readers and viewers. This means that legacy media must rely on—and kowtow to—social media in order to survive. With this in mind, I argue that social media's own advertising-centric license to do business is a logical addition to Herman and Chomsky's second filter.[49]

The third filter, the sourcing of mass media news, is more complicated in the social media era. Social media firms, like traditional media companies, are also "drawn into a symbiotic relationship with powerful sources of information by economic necessity and reciprocity of interest."[50] But the means by which this happens are slightly different than with legacy mass media. In fact, social media generally rely on traditional media firms—which, as Herman and Chomsky described, follow the ruling interests represented by myriad PR firms armed with press releases—to provide their users with content. Indeed, this is how they attempt to wriggle out of the charge that they are media companies and thus subject to regulation. But the thing that classifies social media companies as media companies, full stop, is the fact that social media firms use purpose-built algorithms to determine how information gets to people, exactly who gets it, and when. They source their news from traditional media, but they shape how that news is disseminated and to whom. Algorithms, as many have argued, are loaded with the social and cultural hang-ups of their builders.[51] They are intended to curate and dictate the flow of information in ways particular to company interests. The change to Herman and Chomsky's third filter, then, is to include the crucial role of dissemination algorithms today; the third filter should now be the sourcing and algorithmic curation of mass media news.

The fourth filter, flak and enforcers, still applies in the social media era, for the complex relationship between major social media firms and the powers they serve—advertisers, governments, and other powerful entities—mirrors that of legacy mass media firms. Flak, Herman and Chomsky explain, "refers to negative responses to a media statement of program."[52] Basically, it lies in the ability to threaten the bottom line of media firms by complaining about or marshaling threats of punishment for a given media product. Flak, they argue, can deter media companies from stating specific facts, taking certain positions, or airing particular programs. The most damaging flak comes from the powerful—those that can either indirectly or directly levy serious lawsuits or use threats of regulation to control media firms.

Although it looks a little different now than it did in 1988, flak still plays a role in the propaganda of the digital age. Massive companies like Unilever (which owns Dove, Ben & Jerry's, and many other brands) have, with the backing of groups like the Anti-Defamation League and the NAACP, pulled advertising from Facebook, Instagram, and Twitter in a bid to force these companies to address systemic problems, including those perpetuated by computational propaganda.[53] But other powerful interests exert their will over social media firms for much less noble-seeming goals. India, until recently heralded as the world's largest democracy, has begun to backslide toward authoritarianism under the rule of Narendra Modi and his BJP.

As discussed in chapter 1, Indians are voracious users of social media, particularly WhatsApp and Facebook, and propagandists are sowing disinformation at unprecedented scales using the huge reach of these platforms. (India has the largest state-bounded group of Facebook users in the world, with an audience of 290 million—100 million more users than log on from the United States.)[54] How might Modi and the BJP leverage flak to get Facebook to prioritize or downplay particular content? Facebook has drawn a great deal of scrutiny for its connections to the BJP, which critics say are motivating Facebook's lack of action to prevent the hate, disinformation, and propaganda flowing from the BJP's IT cells to India's massive user base.[55] Flak, especially from powerful groups, is as much a controlling factor in the propaganda and broader communications of social media firms today as it has traditionally been for legacy media companies.

Herman and Chomsky wrote the first version of *Manufacturing Consensus* at the tail end of the Cold War, just a few years before the eventual success of perestroika and dismantling of the Soviet Union in 1991. Their second edition was written just as China became a market economy, embracing capitalism and softening its communist economic stance. The fifth filter they include in these versions of the book, anticommunism as a control measure, was a product of the anticommunist attitudes that pervaded the West in both 1988 and 2002. Today, in many ways, communism is less relevant for this purpose than socialism. During the 2020 U.S. election, for instance, our research team at the University of Texas tracked numerous allegations of socialism levied against Joe Biden and other democratic candidates. In most circumstances, this false allegation was delivered in Spanish, geared toward stoking fear among Latin Americans who had left socialist autocracies in Cuba and Venezuela for the United States, and some of it sought to pit U.S. Latinos against Black Lives Matter groups.[56] These charges of socialism were pure propaganda—much of it spread via chat applications like WhatsApp.

Much has changed since 2002, but Russia and China remain the primary and perhaps most useful specters of control for those in power in the West. Many of the documented computational propaganda campaigns have been framed as originating in either Russia or China. For example, the role of computational propaganda in the 2016 U.S. election, the 2016 Brexit referendum, the 2019 elections in Mozambique (as well as a slew of other African contests and events), and the 2019 protests in Colombia (and across South America) has been documented by and large through the lens of the threat posed by Russian propaganda.[57] This fear is to some degree rooted in fact: Russia's online propaganda activities occur in conjunction with Russian state-controlled mass media firms RT and Sputnik, both of which have an ever-growing international presence, and China has similarly used both digital and broadcast-based channels to spread its own state-centric propaganda in Hong Kong, Taiwan, Tibet, and, increasingly, within Europe and the United States.[58] The Western media has, unsurprisingly, vigorously responded to each and all of these campaigns with anti-Russian and anti-Chinese sentiment.

In the modern era, this fifth filter is no longer specifically about the Cold War–era fears of communism documented by Herman and Chomsky. It is not even specifically about the now-pervasive concern about socialism, which has somehow come to mean the same thing in the popular imagination. Now, the fifth filter must be broadened to include fear of the foreigner, the terrorist, or simply the opposition. After the 9/11 terror attacks and subsequent wars in Iraq and Afghanistan, the mass media framed many of its stories in terms of fears about so-called Islamic or anti-Christian terrorists, and social media trends reflected and intensified this framing.[59] With the recent election of illiberal politicians in the United States, Philippines, Hungary, Brazil, India, and several other countries, the powerful no longer attack only overt and declared foreign enemies but also their domestic detractors—real and perceived. The propaganda spread by social and mass media firms focuses more on a particular opposition in a given country or on cultural circumstance (such as the GOP's recent war on what it calls "critical race theory") than on terrorism or communism—though stoking fears of a given candidate's allegedly "socialist" leanings is still a frequent feature of modern campaigns. This shift has brought into sharp focus fears about the polarization produced by computational propaganda and social media disinformation.[60]

My research suggests that besides updating Herman and Chomsky's five existing filters, we should add a sixth. It is this filter that most significantly modernized the existing propaganda model, fitting it for the digital age: we need to add a filter addressing bots, sockpuppets, and other forms of digital "astroturfing"—top-down manipulation efforts purposely designed to look like they come from general users or via genuine "grassroots" political organizing. This sixth filter takes account of today's propaganda in its "computational" or "networked" state. In the 2002 edition of *Manufacturing Consent*, Chomsky and Herman pointed to the problems likely to arise in an Internet-centric media system, but they were writing before social media really began its meteoric rise. (For example, Facebook did not come into widespread public use until at least the mid-2000s.) The addition of this sixth filter accounts for the myriad ways the rise of social media has altered the propaganda system, which is now more complex and chaotic than even Ellul could have imagined.

When we consider bots, sockpuppets, and other forms of digital astroturfing as a filter, we take into account how information is laundered by way of automated tools, anonymous online profiles, and other means of promoting the inorganic flow of politically motivated messaging. The information we encounter on social media is often skewed by a combination of digital tools and algorithmic processes. Elite actors, states and militaries, and all manner of other social media users exploit well-known gaps, flaws, and work-arounds on social media websites using standard social media advertising and communication mechanisms. According to the people I've talked to over the years, particularly political bot builders and propagandists, they generally do this in order to get their perspectives to the masses. They want to give their particularly partisan version of the "truth" more gravitas. They want their ideas to be more accepted and palatable. They want to manufacture consensus.

The Three Levels of Manufacturing Consensus

Today, there are three types of manufactured consensus—all interconnected, a kind of ouroboros of manipulative information—and at the center of the circle are the computational automated tools made available by the rise of social media and the social shift toward digitalism. The three types are

Political-bot-, sockpuppet-, and partisan-nanoinfluencer-based: Automated and human-run, social media–based communication tools geared toward giving the illusion of popularity or opposition to ideas, people, and so on.

Social-media-algorithm-, recommendation-, and trend-based: Social media recommendations and trends that are presented by firms and the news media as accurately reflecting popular opinion but are in fact gameable by way of computational propaganda and other mechanisms.

News-media-based: News organizations' use of content from computational propaganda tools (bots, sockpuppets, and partisan nanoinfluencers) and social media trends as evidence of popular opinion, and their tendency to reproduce, recurate, and further launder content.

Perceptions of propaganda from previous scholars were largely premised on a top-down model, with those at the top dictating what those at the bottom see, hear, and believe. While Ellul challenged this notion, touching on the possibility of a more "egalitarian" sociotechnical form of propaganda, his thinking was understandably bounded by the broadcast-era technology that existed then. Because social media had not yet "democratized" media production, Ellul's sociological view of propaganda was still limited by the idea that elites are the primary producers.

Broadcast media was not as hospitable to individuals wishing to publicize their politically biased beliefs, but as the first type of manufactured consensus shows, it is now possible for anyone with knowledge of social media and a little coding skill to use bots, sockpuppets, and partisan nanoinfluencers to sway opinion. Bots allow almost anyone with access to a computer and the internet to manipulate the flow of information on social media at scale, which in turn produces the conditions for the second and third types of manufactured consensus. Refugio, a political PR guru based in Mexico, repeatedly said that his goal was not just to get people to read the content that a given fake profile spread but to get hundreds or thousands of bots or sockpuppets to alter trends or recommendations in such a way that even more people saw the content—and saw it through the lens of trusted, legitimate content pushed by a social media firm. Once the content was legitimized by the social media infrastructure, news media commonly picked up a given trend as a story and reported on it.

How Consensus Is Manufactured

According to many of the people I interviewed for this research project, including bot herders and campaign personnel, the goals and tactics of bot- and sockpuppet-driven computational propaganda are not focused and coherent. In fact, bots specifically are often seen simply as "one tool among many" in digital campaign efforts defined by a common ethos of "throwing things against the wall and seeing what sticks." Those who use the tools of computational propaganda most often seek to spur the bandwagon effect, sometimes by (like Refugio) generating fake social media trends with automatically or artificially spread hashtags, and at other times using bots and anonymous profiles to try to suppress the opinions of the opposition, either through targeted harassment or spam.

Many of my informants did not seem to see (or did not admit that they saw) how bots, sockpuppets, and other tools negatively affect political communication writ large. (This may be because many of them were cagey and defensive about the political and moral legitimacy of using automated, or fake, social media profiles to sway voters.) However, bots make it possible for one person or group to massively enhance their presence online and maximize the effects of their opinions. This is what I mean when I say that bots allow for the democratization (in terms of who can use it) of digital propaganda: they allow the individual to make and disseminate propaganda, rather than reserving that ability to the elite. One informant, a political bot builder, put it this way: if one person operating one profile can automate their profile to tweet every minute, just think what one person running one thousand automated profiles can do. In another way, though, this is antidemocratic, because it provides the tools of amplification and suppression, making it possible for one voice to be counted more heavily in the political conversation than another. As Ellul notes, and as I've observed earlier, we cannot measure direct effects or clear success from these bots—in part because the clearest outcomes of computational propaganda campaigns are often chaos and confusion. But this informational chaos, like direct propagandistic political speech, can undermine the democratic process, producing ambivalence about politics, reluctance to vote, or anger at an invisible or engineered foe.

The concept of manufacturing consensus is drawn from the ways the people I've encountered were using computational propaganda in political circumstances in multiple countries, dating back as early as 2007. In the Americas, political actors in Mexico, Ecuador, Venezuela, and Brazil pioneered the deployment of bots in attempts to boost credibility through increased metrics: follows, likes, retweets, shares, comments, and so on.[61,62,63,64] It was not until the 2016 U.S. election, though, that computational propaganda—specifically, the ways that social media platforms were being used to manufacture consensus around candidates and campaigns—came to the forefront of the global political psyche.[65] Both the tools (in 2016, primarily bots and sockpuppets) and the communication strategies they afforded (disinformation, algorithmic manipulation, boosting of social media metrics) were the lead story for major news outlets from New York to Tokyo.[66,67]

Let us look at a brief case study of how consensus can be manufactured: 2016's U.S. election. During this election, Twitter, Facebook, and other large social media companies (the first filter) played a more central role in candidate and campaign communication than it had in any previous political contest. According to a November 7, 2016, data report from Twitter, "People in the US sent one billion tweets about the election since the primary debates began in August of last year."[68] Both party-nominated candidates, but especially Donald Trump, used Twitter as a frontline communication channel to reach supporters and to attack a seemingly ever-growing opposition (the fifth filter). The Trump campaign's communication strategy was deeply dependent on social media advertising on major social media platforms (the second filter).[69] Firms like Cambridge Analytica,

working first on behalf of Ted Cruz and later for Trump, used advertising to spread a great deal of disinformative content.[70]

Before and during the election, Trump pointed to his Twitter metrics as evidence that he had a backing not being captured
in mainstream polls. But research reveals that communication of
Trump-related content on Twitter was heavily bolstered by bots.[71]
According to my research with Bence Kollanyi and Philip Howard, in the week preceding election day, Twitter bots messaged five
times more in support of Trump then they did for Hillary Clinton. An analysis of major primary candidates' Twitter followings by
FiveThirtyEight found that Trump led the pack in fake followers.[72] A
report of the Twitter analysis tool Twitter Audit corroborated this
assertion, finding that nearly half of Trump's Twitter following was
fake.[73] Did Trump create his own fake followers? Definitely not. Did
his campaign, their contractors, or subcontractors? We may never
know. What the research makes clear is that there was a significant
amount of computational propaganda geared toward helping Trump
secure the White House. My research suggests that it likely came
from a wide variety of quarters. Yes, Russia spread some of it, but a
great deal of it also came from internal U.S. actors, many of whom
were not officially working for any country or campaign.

A Republican political strategist I call Cassidy, along with several
other professional digital PR experts, repeatedly stressed to me that
candidates and campaigns work constantly to stay up to date on a variety of evolving digital campaigning tools and a constantly changing
communication landscape. Some of these digital tools are simply updated versions of previous campaigns' traditional marketing efforts.
For example, strategists associated with both the 2016 Republican
and Democratic campaigns told me that interactive advertisements,
livestreamed video, memes, and personalized messaging all played a

role in the spread of partisan content during the 2016 election. This is consistent with what other scholars have found. According to Daniel Kreiss, "While campaigns have long had to adapt to changing media environments, the pace, scale, and social consequences of change are qualitatively different in an era of rapid shifts in the application layer of the internet."[74]

Digital tools, including infrastructural aspects of Twitter and Facebook, are primarily used to effect voter turnout. However, many of the people I spoke to about the 2016 U.S. contest told me that elements of social media, including bots, were also used by a variety of groups to achieve other, less conventional goals: to sow confusion, to give a false impression of online support, to attack and defame the opposition, and to spread illegitimate news reports. In short, to create informational chaos.

In the following four chapters, I examine the major groups who drive the manufacture of consensus and contribute to this informational chaos. I detail how governments—some of the most powerful entities to leverage computational propaganda—use political bots and other tools to further their goals and to stymie their opposition. I explain how the ability to propagandize has opened up a new type of propaganda actor, the *automated digital constituent*, which is made possible by bots. I discuss the role of social media and big tech in all of this: how have their decisions (or indecision) around trending/ recommendation algorithms and a variety of other issues helped to produce the propaganda ecosystem as we know it today? Finally, I unpack how journalists play into this new landscape, showing how they work to combat propaganda and disinformation, how they are targeted by it, and how they (unwittingly) help to spread it.

3

State Use of Computational Propaganda

Rafael Correa, the former president of Ecuador, was notoriously willing to use any and all media tools at his disposal to cement his rule. During his tenure, the Ecuadorian media system became much more restricted, and both state-funded and private media operated as his attack dogs, regularly savaging other, less supportive media outlets.[1] In early 2020, Correa was convicted of corruption charges stemming from his ten years as president and sentenced to eight years in prison.[2] The one-time leader now boasts his own spot, *Conversations with Correa,* on Russia's state broadcast service RT Spanish. On his show, he interviews current and former Latin American politicians, including Nicolás Maduro, the dictator of Venezuela, and celebrities such as filmmaker Oliver Stone.

I have family from Ecuador, and they know that I study computational propaganda. When Correa was in power, I used to receive regular messages from them detailing his government's latest online machinations, which ranged from direct surveillance and hacking attacks to "soft" attacks on the opposition via automation on social media. In 2015, a conversation with my family prompted me to write a report about the Ecuadorian government's role in the #HackingTeam leaks, which revealed that the regime had spent millions of dollars on malware and surveillance technology.[3] When several Ecuadorian websites, including the site of the media freedom group Fundación Mil Hojas, published stories on the Correa government's activities associated with Hacking Team, the sites were shut down through direct denial of service attacks shortly after they published the material.

In addition to these back-end hacking tactics, Correa and his cronies used social media, including political bots and pro-government trolls, to destabilize opponents. In conversations with other Ecuadorians, including technology experts and journalists, I learned that Correa's government regularly used social media sites—particularly Twitter and Facebook—to attack their opposition (Correa called the operators behind these attacks his "defamers"). According to my informants, accounts that were obviously automated regularly played a role in these propaganda efforts. During and prior to 2015, "streams of pro-government propaganda, anti-opposition trolls, and hashtag spamming" came together to form what my interviewees called "Twitter Gate."[4] I was told that this group of online offensives, whose roots went back as far as 2012, originated in several physical Ecuadorian "troll centers" similar to those used by Russia's Internet Research Agency (IRA).

These social media attacks often sought to silence Correa's critics. For example, in 2014 there was a set of coordinated attacks against Correa critics by Twitter bots and sockpuppet accounts. Later that year, the Twitter accounts of a number of Correa's opponents were suspended, and research later revealed that the suspensions had been pushed by Ximah Digital CEO Juan Carlos Vascones, a Correa supporter who also acted as Twitter's Ecuadorian representative. As I wrote then: "Both Vascones and Ximah Digital are associated with Ribeney SA, a private company that allegedly serves as a social media troll center in the capital city of Quito. Official documents prove that Ecuador's Ministry of Strategic Sectors signed a 'social media strategy' contract with Ribeney in 2013."[5] Correa and his government, with the help of Vascones and a cadre of social media "marketing consultants," had built a reasonably sophisticated state-sponsored trolling apparatus. In 2015, they extended the apparatus, inviting private citizens to become "defamers": Correa launched Somos+, a website where his supporters could subscribe to alerts about people "smearing" the government on social media and respond in kind.

Governmental Bot Use: The Tip of the Iceberg

When I first began studying the political use of bots as a doctoral student at the University of Washington, I was particularly focused on how national governments—including their militaries, intelligence services, and broader bureaucratic arms—leveraged bots over social media for their own propagandistic means and ends. This interest had grown out of several news articles I had read about Twitter bot use during the Arab Spring. The first article I remember seeing, from 2011, described a multi-country online clash over social media between protestors and their human and bot detractors. As free expression activist Jillian C. York wrote, in Bahrain, Iran, Morocco, Syria, "pro-revolution users of [Twitter] have found themselves locked in a battle of the hashtags as . . . accounts with a pro-government message are quickly created to counter the prevailing narrative."[6] According to York, the clearest case of Twitter bots being used to perpetuate pro-government ends was taking place in Syria. Pro-democracy users on Twitter were using the hashtags #Syria, #Daraa, and #Mar15 to organize and garner attention for their movements, but suddenly the hashtags were barraged with pro-government messages that seemed to come from bots. As Syrian blogger Anas Qtiesh explained, "These accounts were believed to be manned by Syrian *mokhabarat* [intelligence] agents with poor command of both written Arabic and English, and an endless arsenal of bite and insults."[7] Later research verified these claims.[8]

York's article inspired me to write my first paper on global media reports alleging that states were using political bots.[9] I'd heard about bots being used on Twitter for all sorts of seemingly beneficial, and even funny, reasons, but growing accounts of governmental use intrigued and worried me. With this in mind, I created a global dataset of bot events that coded for the locations of political bots, their number and growth, and the strategy behind their deployment. The report offered definitions and descriptions of political bot use overall as well as specifics of each state's individual strategies and tactics. I found news reports alleging state use of political bots—governmentally sanctioned computational propaganda—in eighteen countries. Later, my former colleagues at the Oxford Internet Institute continued similar work but with a broader eye toward media reports and other evidence of state use of "cyber troops" and "organized social media manipulation." In their 2019 report on the subject, they found "evidence of organized social media manipulation campaigns which have taken place in 70 countries, up from 48 countries in 2018 and 28 countries in 2017." They wrote that this state-sponsored manipulation "involves building an inventory of the evolving strategies, tools, and techniques of computational propaganda, including the use of 'political bots' to amplify hate speech or other forms of manipulated content, the illegal harvesting of data or micro-targeting, or deploying an army of 'trolls' to bully or harass political dissidents or journalists online."[10] Their research made it evident that states were indeed using bots and other automated, algorithmic, and human-based strategies of online politicking, and that the practice was in fact growing.

This chapter is about these state producers of computational propaganda—about how some of the most powerful political actors on the planet use computational propaganda to entrench their own power while simultaneously working to confuse, splinter, and silence their opposition.[11] The core concept in this chapter—and the subject of its first half—is *state-sponsored trolling*: "the [state] use of targeted online hate and harassment campaigns to intimidate and silence individuals critical of the state."[12] This concept grows out of the work of a global network of researchers, many of whom have experienced firsthand this novel, digital form of governmental control.[13] As we will see, many of these trolling campaigns across the globe used political bots as key tools for amplifying or suppressing particular voices, and I report my own conversations with people who both constructed and experienced state-sponsored trolling campaigns.

The second half of the chapter discusses how governments benefit not only from state-sponsored trolling but from other types of computational propaganda. I detail how the broader infrastructure of social media—which has always enabled the use of bots because of its core principles of anonymity and automation—functions as a support infrastructure for partisan computational propaganda. As I show, many candidates, campaigns, and causes supported by computational propaganda benefit from the manufacture of consensus. Sometimes, these beneficiaries do not directly initiate digital propaganda campaigns or approve the use of political bots. Other times, the connections between the political bots and the governments, people, or ideas they are championing seems closer—although it always remains difficult to prove.

State Use of Computational Propaganda: State-Sponsored Trolling

In 2014 and 2015 I spent some time in Hungary as a graduate research fellow at the Center for Media, Data, and Society at Central European University in Budapest. At the time, I was working to figure out whether computational propaganda in Hungary was being deployed in ways similar to those in Ukraine and other Eastern European countries. There was clear evidence from a variety of sources that Russian governmental actors were using social media, particularly political bots, to attack pro-Ukrainian users and to spread pro-Russian narratives among Ukrainian users.[14] It seemed that these pro-Russian narratives were also being bolstered by groups from inside Ukraine. Was Viktor Orbán, the fascist-leaning and pro-Russian prime minister of Hungary, also leveraging or benefiting from similar digital campaigns?

After months of research, including both quantitative analyses of Hungarian social media data and interviews with Hungarian digital activists, digital PR gurus, and others, we came to the conclusion that neither Orbán and his cronies—nor Russian government agents—were leveraging computational propaganda to boost their causes in any way we could track. The inability to accurately trace any influence may have been related to the fact that Orbán had (and still has, at the time this book goes to press) a stranglehold on traditional media in the country. As Dr. Philip Howard, then the director of the Center for Media, Data and Society, wrote in the *New York Times*, Orbán was working to build "Europe's most controlled media system."[15] At the time, Orbán's relatively small state government didn't seem to need social media to troll its people.

My team and I hit a dead end in Hungary, where the manufacture of consent was playing out through traditional media channels rather than computational propaganda. But, we thought, perhaps people in other nearby countries were experiencing state-backed computational propaganda? A new colleague and office-mate named Isa, who has a deep knowledge of media, politics, and the Middle East, arrived at Central European University. I told her that we'd run into a dead end looking for computational propaganda in Hungary and that I was looking elsewhere. "Have you thought about looking at things in Turkey?" she asked. Istanbul was just a short, cheap, direct plane ride away. Media reports suggested that citizens there, including journalists and prominent opposition activists, were reeling from a series of social media attack campaigns.[16] It seemed that President Recep Tayyip Erdoğan and his government were not very secretive about using political bots and other digital strategies to attack their opponents.[17]

Isa pointed out some Turkish news articles on political bot use in the country and helped me with translations. I quickly found information on several people who seemed to have a hand in government-sponsored automated Twitter attacks. Even more interestingly, I found details about a group in the country who were fighting back against the government's computational propaganda campaign using the same tactics: allegedly, they too were using bots to amplify their attacks. I did some fairly simple open-source intelligence work online and managed to track down names and e-mails of people working for both groups. I sent out cold e-mails explaining my project and crossed my fingers. This was early days, and I still hadn't had a great deal of luck getting prominent political bot builders to talk to me. After all, I thought, why would they want to talk to a researcher writing about people using social media to manipulate and attack others for political reasons?

I got two responses. One was from a "social media expert" who was known to work for the Erdoğan government. News articles and other online information I could find about him described him as the go-to Twitter and Facebook marketing person for Erdoğan's Justice and Development Party. The other was from Haluk, an opposition digital activist. He was an IT professional who had also been profiled by local Turkish media as a staunch anti-Erdoğan activist. In correspondence, both of them openly shared that, in addition to using social media for traditional types of political advertising, they used

Twitter bots to spread political content on behalf of their respective parties—information that they had also shared with the Turkish press. It seemed that the media reports suggesting that more than eighteen thousand bot accounts were tweeting in favor of Erdoğan were correct, as were those reporting that people were fighting back against the pro-Erdoğan bots with their own.[18,19] I decided it was time to go to Istanbul.

While in Budapest I had made a couple of friends from Turkey, and they offered to introduce me to their friends and contacts, many of whom worked in and around politics and media. Over the course of my two trips to Istanbul, and via e-mail, video calls, and the phone, I was able to talk to several people who either worked within the Erdoğan governmental orbit or actively participated in groups fighting against the current regime. Everyone I spoke to made it clear that most politically involved people in Turkey, particularly those who regularly used social media, knew that the state government and other politicians in the country used political trolling tactics online to attack the opposition and extol the virtues of the state. Some also knew about the use of political bots and sockpuppet accounts, saying that anyone on Twitter in Turkey at the time would encounter social media bots and anonymous accounts getting political.

The stories regarding these strategies were verified by International Press Institute research, which detailed the Turkish government's state-sponsored trolling apparatus and confirmed its use of political bots and other illicit social media control tactics.[20] The group followed governmental manipulation and harassment campaigns over the course of three tumultuous years, from 2013 to 2016—a period that included 2013's Gezi Park protests and 2016's failed coup d'état. Reports on prolonged, multifaceted Turkish computational propaganda campaigns featured discussions of the use of political bots and sockpuppet-led trolling campaigns. During this time, government officials and pro-government media pundits used their significant social media presence to openly attack several well-known journalists who had reported stories that cast the government in a negative light. Indeed, as a result of the campaign, the journalists received death and rape threats. The Turkish state-sponsored trolling campaign was a sophisticated, coordinated propaganda offense that took place both offline and online and included numerous key features of the propaganda model.

Turkey and Ecuador were some of the first governments to use computational propaganda. Now, many other governments around the world regularly use social media to attack journalists, opposition politicians, and even their own citizens. Government propaganda and trolling campaigns take place on nearly every prominent social media site or application, including Twitter, YouTube, WhatsApp, and many others. Facebook and Reddit are particularly fertile ground for computational propaganda; countless online propaganda experts have explained to me over the years that they use Facebook, particularly the "groups" feature, to spam citizens with pro-government messaging and vitriol, and they use Reddit to find and silence opposition activists. A few people in an office in St. Petersburg, Ankara, or Quito can run thousands of automated social media accounts and hundreds of human-run ones, and those who are attacked by these bots think that they face armies of real detractors.

One such professional state-sponsored troll is Andres Sepulveda, who is currently serving a ten-year sentence in Colombia for using online political manipulation during that country's 2014 presidential election.[21] According to a story from Bloomberg, backed up by information from my fieldwork and reports from many interviewees for this book project, Sepulveda worked on a number of projects for various Latin American governments and political candidates, who paid him large sums of money to use computational propaganda to manipulate communication and public opinion during presidential elections in Colombia, Costa Rica, El Salvador, Guatemala, Honduras, Mexico, Nicaragua, Panama, and Venezuela. He used social media bots run by small groups of people to amplify content supporting the candidates for whom he worked while simultaneously suppressing and drowning out information from the opposition. As the extensive Bloomberg report noted, Sepulveda and his team were working to hack public opinion—in my terms, to manufacture consensus. They used bots and other social media tools to create the illusion of popularity for various prominent politicians, candidates, or causes. I've spoken to other propagandists, particularly in Mexico, who back up Sepulveda's claims, and these people say that he was simply one such hireling among many.

In the course of my research I have learned that governmental actors in Ecuador, Mexico, Russia, Turkey, and Venezuela have worked with various organized state-sponsored trolling entities. Some were "in house," operating from directly within the government, and others were paid contractors—operators like Sepulveda or firms like Ribeney SA. The work of scholars Nicholas Monaco, Carly Nyst, and their collaborators breaks down these state-sponsored trolling operations into four "mechanisms of state responsibility": (1) state-executed, (2) state-directed or -coordinated, (3) state-incited or -fueled, and (4) state-leveraged or -endorsed.[22]

At the top of this hierarchy are the campaigns that come directly from within the government of a given country. Monaco and Nyst point to Azerbaijan, China, Russia, and Turkey as users of these sort of directly state-funded "cyber militias," and I've identified similar online militias in Brazil and India in the course of my research. At the bottom of the hierarchy are campaigns seemingly begun by people who are not affiliated with the state—"grassroots" campaigns that states then leverage for their own ends. In these cases, "governments point to the existence of seemingly independent groundswells of public opinion [on social media] to justify and legitimate state positions."[23] For example, the Chinese, Filipino, and Indian governments have pointed to alleged online support from regular citizens to justify the government's social media attacks on journalists, opposition members, and even foreigners. Similarly, Indian prime minister Narendra Modi and Filipino president Rodrigo Duterte have both directly endorsed this form of state-sponsored trolling, both through their own social media accounts and through posts by bloggers who are friendly to their regimes.

The middle area—state-directed and state-incited campaigns—is where most state-sponsored trolling and computational propaganda campaigns occur. In state-directed campaigns, governments pay for and coordinate bot-driven propaganda and other forms of political trolling. Venezuela's Maduro has made use of these tactics, directing contractors to attack and defame his opponents over the encrypted chat applications Telegram and WhatsApp, as well as on unencrypted social media sites. Another example of this type of second-tier operation is Ecuador's use of Ribeney SA's bots and trolls. The third mechanism, state-incited trolling, is, according to Monaco and Nyst, "the most pernicious" of all state-sponsored social media propaganda operations. In these circumstances, "the government maintains an arm's-length distance from the attack but nevertheless both instigates and profits from it."[24] My own experiences back this up—governments often don't want to be directly implicated in either computational propaganda or trolling campaigns, for obvious reasons, but these campaigns appear to have powerful effects. Monaco and Nyst point to the United States as an example of this. They write that Donald Trump and his government have been known to provoke social media trolling campaigns, working through former presidential adviser Steve Bannon and using Breitbart news and other far-right platforms, to sic adherents on particular targets.

State-sponsored trolling and computational propaganda are not used only by authoritarian or illiberal regimes. Governmental actors in Western democracies (some of which have admittedly moved toward illiberalism in recent years) also leverage political bots and other tools for sowing today's propaganda. During my research I've spoken to many political marketing strategists in the United States and United Kingdom who specialize in digital campaigning. Several have unabashedly told me they've worked on political campaigns, and for politicians, that have used bots both to boost their social media follows and likes and to bolster their image. Cassidy, one such interviewee, continues to work at a high level within the U.S. Republican Party. He and another Republican strategist called Eastwood told me that they were familiar with the practice of using social bots for political purposes. They were quick to point out, though, that bots were just one part of a larger arsenal of political communication tools. Both suggested that methods for buying and deploying political bots were shadowed, hidden away in the depths of political consulting efforts rather than directly tied to official campaigns and their staffs. More often than not, they told me, those campaigns benefited from or leveraged supporters' existing bot-driven smear or disinformation efforts. My broader experiences studying U.S. and U.K. government-related use of political bots echoes this. Most of the time, it was the entire web of social media, including both underlying infrastructure like algorithms and bots launched by a wide array of paid and unpaid groups, that benefited politicians like Donald Trump.

Computational propaganda also links up with traditional media campaigns in "networked" spin campaigns, highlighting the interconnection of old and new propaganda strategies.[25] These marriages of old and new media propaganda are common in Venezuela, Turkey, and Russia. And in the United States, the cable "news" channel One America News Network (OAN) often regurgitates conspiracy theories and disinformation that are first cooked up online. While OAN may not have a high viewership compared with major networks like Fox or CNN, they do have the ear of Donald Trump and his advisers. According to the *New York Times,* "Thanks to one powerful viewer in the White House, the network's influence—and its conspiracy theories—are echoing in the highest reaches of American politics."[26]

How States and Politicians Benefit from Bots, Sockpuppets, and Traditional Media Propaganda

On the evening of November 8, 2016, Manhattan was uncharacteristically quiet. At 10 p.m., I walked from an election return watch party at an office in the Flatiron District to my hotel a few blocks north in Chelsea. Looking through the windows of shops, bars, and restaurants on Sixth Avenue, I saw crowds of people with eyes glued to TV screens, many playing Fox News. I passed by a crowd of laughing Indian American men wearing "Make America Great Again" hats and carrying both Indian and American flags. Republican candidate Donald Trump had begun to shift toward the lead in the swing states—Florida, Ohio, Michigan, Wisconsin, and Pennsylvania. My contacts at the Javits Center, where Hillary Clinton was hosting her election night gathering, told me that the scene had changed markedly from the jubilation and confidence of just an hour before. People were beginning to leave in droves, and several of the scheduled speakers had reportedly not taken the stage. The candidate herself was notably absent. Around 2:30 a.m., the Associated Press called Wisconsin for Trump, and with this, projected that he would win the election. It would, without a doubt, go down as one of the most unexpected presidential victories in U.S. history.

Most pundits, pollsters, and political scientists had been wrong in their predictions of a strong Clinton victory. The day after the election, GOP strategist and "Never-Trumper" Mike Murphy wrote on Twitter, "I've believed in data for 30 years and data died tonight. I could not have been more wrong about this election."[27] Months later, statistician Nate Silver, whose website FiveThirtyEight had given Clinton a three-times greater chance to win than Trump, would disagree with the widespread sentiment that the election spelled the "death of data" in politics. In an interview with the *Harvard Gazette*, Silver said, "One thing I think is a myth is the notion of, 'Oh, polls got the election wrong.' I do not think that's true at all. The polls pointed toward a competitive race. . . . I think it more reflects blind spots in people's thinking."[28] Throughout the last months of the election, Trump and his campaign staff were dismissive—correctly, it seems—of media narratives and poll numbers that suggested they were far behind.

Retrospectively, this "upset" victory can't be explained by something as simple as data being flawed, polls being wrong, or media groupthink causing imagined consensus about a Clinton victory. In reality, the landscape—in terms of both data and sociocultural perspectives on the election—was incredibly complicated. Assumptions about Democratic party prowess in the media tended to ignore the inner mechanics of the Electoral College—and, perhaps more damaging, they also ignored the power of the conservative media ecosystem.[29] Pollsters and journalists failed to translate the ways in which a 30 percent chance of victory for Trump and consistently close national polling averages were in fact signals that the race was statistically much less than certain. They ignored the numbers on social media, particularly on Twitter, and across conservative news outlets, all of which showed a different election.

On Twitter, Trump consistently received a larger market share of attention than Clinton, and his interaction metrics on the site—follower numbers, retweets, mentions, and likes—outpaced those of his Democratic rival.[30,31] Trump himself regularly pointed to his Twitter popularity as a factor in his win. In a March 2017 interview with Fox News's Tucker Carlson, Trump said, "I wouldn't be here if it was not for Twitter."[32] But if something was not quite right about the survey data public pollsters used to predict a Clinton win, the Twitter data referred to by Trump was also seriously flawed in reflecting actual candidate popularity. Research by Yu Wang and colleagues that showed "Trumpists" on Twitter as being more engaged and more influential than "Clintonists" relied on face-value reports—on how many people followed those Trump followers—to calculate their influence.[33] Republicans, including Trump himself, did the same thing, pointing out simple follower numbers in claims about Twitter as a marker of public appeal. In January 2017, CNN ran an entire story about the then-president-elect reaching 20 million followers, in which reporter Brian Stelter wrote, "The president-elect brings up his social media stats on a regular basis, adding up the users who follow him on Twitter, Facebook and Instagram to say he reaches 46 million people through the three sites."[34]

In the same story, however, Stelter made a crucial note: "The total [number of Trump Twitter followers], while impressive, is belied by the fact, like many social media users, Trump has some followers that are either robots (known as 'bots') or dormant users who never see what he posts." In fact, both bot detection tools and the researchers who use them suggest that Trump's overall follower numbers on social media were around 50 percent fake in 2016—and that Clinton had a similarly high number of bot followers on Twitter.[35,36]

Because swathes of bots follow political candidates and drive up metrics (likes, hashtags, retweets, replies), the use of Twitter as a measure for political support is inherently flawed. However, this is not to say that Twitter cannot affect political support. As I have been arguing, bots *do* have influence on perceptions of a candidate's political cachet, across both traditional media and public opinion. Media outlets regularly refer to Twitter—and Twitter metrics—when deciding on what story to report, and bots on sites like Twitter can be useful propaganda tools for getting stories into the traditional media ecosystems and helping to manufacture consensus.[37] Social media bots and related tools play a significant role in altering the flow of information online: as Chris Wells and colleagues have shown, "Social media activity, in the form of retweets of candidate posts, provided a significant boost to news media coverage of Trump, but no comparable boost for other candidates"; in 2016, more bots tweeted in support of Trump than Clinton during pivotal moments of the election; and the Trump bots were more successful at garnering engagement from influential figures.[38,39]

According to a 2020 article in *Nature* examining conversations about migration from northern Africa to Italy, "social bots play a central role in the exchange of significant content."[40] Media companies regularly report on stories that begin as computational propaganda, and people in positions of power—such as politicians and celebrity influencers—share bot content on their accounts.[41] For instance, during the 2016 U.S. presidential election, candidates, campaigns, and campaign associates used and interacted with (retweeted, liked, followed, etc.) bots, sockpuppets, and computational propaganda content, and like other politicians around the globe, they continue to do so.[42]

While received wisdom suggests that the most invasive political bots, disinformation, and computational propaganda during the 2016 U.S. campaign came from the Russian government or groups such as the Alt-right or Antifa, my own work and the work of many others suggest that mainstream political campaigns, their subcontractors, and their supporters in the United States use—indeed, rely on—propaganda from digital tools. The propagandistic content begins online, then spreads through regular users to contacts across their social networks and then into traditional media channels. Its appearance in the legacy media gives the propaganda an even stronger illusion of popularity and significance—the manufacture of consensus at work.

Conclusion

As this chapter has shown, governments are among the most well-resourced producers of computational propaganda and the greatest beneficiaries of it, whether they intentionally leverage or passively benefit from it. State-sponsored trolling strategies to silence and intimidate opposition often rely on large groups of human users and political bots to amplify the harassment, and it is common for online propaganda campaigns that began as government-led offensives to be picked up by ordinary people who fervently believe in the government's causes. It is also common for governments to directly pay or indirectly compensate cyber militias that operate both real social media profiles and sockpuppet accounts to carry out these state-sponsored trolling campaigns, harassing detractors and sowing effusive support for the government. Finally, governments' own official propaganda efforts leverage seemingly organic groundswells of criticism that come from ordinary people, some of whom may simply be expressing their authentic political opinions and others who may themselves be intentionally producing computational propaganda for their own ends. This interleaved, multilayered use of social media as a tool for propaganda can incorporate apps and sites like Telegram and YouTube to spread both overt governmental messaging and covert disinformation or spin.

Government-sponsored propaganda campaigns are an entire connected ecosystem—a propaganda ouroboros in which online campaigns shade into and grow out of legacy media campaigns and news coverage. In Ecuador, Turkey, the United States, and many other places, what begins on social media spreads to traditional media and back again. When states hold interests in traditional media and can leverage both soft and hard control, politicians and governmental employees can legitimize computational propaganda efforts and information operations by translating them to radio, newspapers, and elsewhere. This is particularly true in authoritarian states with a stranglehold on their countries' media systems, but it is also increasingly true in democratic states—notably Brazil, India, and the United States, as the work of Yochai Benkler and colleagues on the 2016 U.S. elections shows.[43]

Although states spend the most resources on and reap the most benefits from computational propaganda campaigns, they are far from the only actors to use digital forms of propaganda to manufacture consensus. In the next chapter, I describe an emergent group of consensus manufacturers: what I call *automated digital influencers.* These individuals and small groups generally act outside the purview of (and without the support of) better-resourced groups like states, corporations, and the like, but they are able to harness the power of social media to spread their own forms of propaganda. With the help of bots, sockpuppets, and loosely organized coalitions of like-minded individuals, they are able to scale their campaigns in ways that get them noticed. Many of the informants I've talked to over the years have proudly shared "wins" in which they were able to get "mainstream" media to report on their content or politicians to tweet it; traditional media is central to the automated digital influencers' efforts—perhaps even more central than to states' campaigns—and for many of them, the biggest win they can achieve is to see one of their bespoke disinformation yarns appear in a major news story or NGO report.

4

Automated Political Influencers

Budapest is a city of contradictions. Its name is a portmanteau of the two very different cities (Buda and Pest) that form the current Hungarian capital. Buda is known for its relatively peaceful rolling hills and sophistication, while Pest is flat and businesslike, home to most of the city's tourism and nightlife. Split by the Danube River, the city's two halves are home to a simultaneously jarring and beautiful combination of Baroque, Classical, Art Nouveau, and Brutalist architecture. Massive blocks of Soviet-era concrete flats sit alongside the ornate edifices of early twentieth-century banks, theaters, hotels, and shops. Ottoman influence abuts European cosmopolitanism alongside the heritage of the Magyar tribes that left the Urals to settle the region. The city sits within the European Union, likely the world's strongest democratic partnership, but it is home to the Hungarian Parliament, overseen by Prime Minister Viktor Orbán— a right-wing nationalist who has openly called for a shift toward illiberalism as he pushes his county into authoritarianism.[1]

János, one of the first people I interviewed in my bid to understand online propaganda, lives and works in Budapest. He is a fitting representative of his contradictory and divided home city. I spoke to him in the summer of 2014, while I worked in Budapest as a doctoral research fellow at Central European University. My long talk with János took place inside the communist-retrofitted shell of one of Budapest's Art Nouveau buildings. During our talk, the strangely incongruous setting—the ambivalent, contradictory nature of both the city and the building itself—seemed to crystallize for me the similarly contradictory nature of the internet. János, a onetime market researcher who left to harness his advertising chops in the greener pastures of tech, waxed poetic on the democratic potential of the internet, discussing its use as an organizing tool. However, he also discussed his experiences in the United States doing advertising for major tech firms such as Yahoo, and in these discussions, he pragmatically described the web as a tremendously useful tool for control. For János, both of these uses of the internet, divergent and opposing as they are, relied on *relationships*: how people, particularly social media users, understood themselves alongside and in relation to others. That, he told me, was something that could be manipulated.

János was one of the first people from inside tech to tell me that social bots—automated profiles built to look like "real" users of a given social media application or website—play a big role in online communication. In a rapid-fire, one-sided conversation, he frenetically quoted George Herbert Mead to me, bouncing back and forth between ideas about mimesis and manipulation. Weren't bots just versions of the people that built them? he asked me rhetorically. When they were used to change peoples' perceptions of political events, weren't they just operating within a digital system built to do precisely the same thing but on a larger scale? Are bots really that different from human users in the long run? After all, in Hungary, he noted, politicians didn't need to use social media bots to game the flow of information online—they could use coordinated groups of actual human users to achieve similar ends. Are these the same phenomenon? His mind raced on: who was to say whether this online propaganda was good or bad, democratic or authoritarian?

The Democratization of Propaganda

As I explained in the previous chapter, in my early days of studying computational propaganda, I focused most of my attention on state-sponsored propaganda campaigns designed around the use of social bots. I had a preconceived idea of how these automated accounts were being used, which was based on what I'd read about the Arab Spring: I thought that bot campaigns were mostly being launched by powerful political actors—governments, politicians, or political parties—to manipulate and attack their opposition. But this missed much of the picture. As I've noted, it is still true that elite political entities or actor groups produce the most sophisticated computational propaganda. This is why reports from the Computational Propaganda Project at Oxford continue to focus on state cyber-troop and social media "warfare" apparatuses.[2] It is why Yochai Benkler and colleagues' study of networked propaganda dedicates a significant number of column inches to computational propaganda in the 2016 U.S. election, including the roles played by Russia and by Cambridge Analytica, the data firm that worked for the Trump campaign to very specifically target micro-demographics and automatically serve them tailored political content—a more polite phrase for propaganda.[3] Of course the world's most powerful political adversaries will continue to leverage all of the new and emerging media tools at their disposal to defame, disinform, and coerce their opposition. But I had missed something crucial with my original narrow focus on governments: the fact that the networked nature of the internet ecosystem makes it possible for almost anyone with access to a connected computer to become an amateur propagandist.

This insight is the source of a crucial difference between the discussion of the power of the network that I offer here and previous discussions from other scholars.[4] I argue that much of the internet's power derives from its structure as a decentralized many-to-many information creation system; this structure allows anyone with the platform and tools to be a propagandist. Previous research has noted the web's potential to be both democratic and antidemocratic; here, I focus on how the tools of democratization are being co-opted for control rather than liberation.[5] My goal in this chapter is to show how the media ecosystem that has allowed anyone to be an amateur journalist—or amateur media maker, as with influencers, vloggers, and the like—has also allowed anyone to manipulate the flow of information for their own political ends.

I call these ordinary people *automated political influencers*. While automated political bots have been among their chief tools since at least 2010, these influencers also make use of human and semi-automated labor to inorganically spread political ideas. They use both manually run sockpuppet accounts and so-called cyborg accounts, which use automation to seek targets and then, once the target is engaged, turn the nuanced work of conversation over to a real person.[6]

Originally, I had planned to describe this category of political bot users and politically inclined digital tech users as *civil society groups*. This nomenclature came out of my research around political bot-building in other countries, where I had witnessed well-organized political nonprofits making use of social bots. As my research progressed, however, it became clear that the category of nongovernmental digital propagandists was far larger (and far messier) than could be accounted for by focusing on official NGOs and institutions. This conceptualization did not adequately capture the lion's share of nonstate and nonjournalistic political bot-making that I was seeing. Through research and discussions with colleagues, it became clear that the notion of "civil society" did not really fit what I was seeing.[7] I therefore shifted to the umbrella notion of automated political influencers, which includes the various individuals around the world who use political bots but are not directly connected to campaigns, corporations, or media institutions. I use the word *influencer* to describe these people for two reasons: they are very much in the business of political influence, and they often use the same social media tactics as more traditional digital influencers do.

In today's world, we are witnessing the *democratization of propaganda*. Perhaps this juxtaposition of *democracy* and *propaganda* seems contradictory, but it is deliberate. In its simplest definition, democracy is rule by the people, and as scholars like Walter Lippmann and Edward Bernays observed, propaganda can help to uphold democracy by influencing the will of the people. And the power to influence public will and opinion is now available to nearly anyone with a computer and a little know-how. As propaganda becomes democratized, its creation and dissemination is no longer limited to only powerful political entities, such as states, militaries, parties, intelligence communities, NGOs, special interest groups, and corporations. In the age of social media and bots, propaganda is no longer a top-down system but a many-to-many system.

Yet the democratization of propaganda does not necessarily produce a more functional democracy—quite the opposite, in fact. As we have all likely anecdotally observed in our own online experiences, it creates a lot of noise and chaos, which can actually damage democracy. It seems clear now that the democratizing power of the internet has contributed significantly to our current problems with disinformation and misinformation. In the course of my research, I've regularly talked to disenchanted folks who look longingly back to the time of the nightly news anchor, when they felt they could get semi-objective news from a trusted source—and when it was relatively easy to tell where the propaganda was coming from.

There are, sadly, no easy fixes. The democratization of propaganda, and the noisiness of our modern communication environment, bring up uncomfortable questions about censorship versus free speech, about the marketplace of ideas versus the right to be free from hate speech and deception. And one of the most troubling things about automated political influencers is that their leveraging of political bots and other digital tools often drowns out exactly the types of nuanced conversations we need to have.

Many of the automated political influencers I've spoken to build bots to spread their own political perspectives. For these makers, the bot is amplifying their own voice, and it is an extension of themselves. This is not an entirely new concept; in previous work, my colleagues and I have argued that in general, people's use of social media bots (whether for comedy, art, work, etc.) reveals that bots are proxies for—separate but intimately tied to—their creators.[8] Other researchers have described a similar sort of symbiotic agency, "informed by the imagined affordances of emerging technology," between bots and their creators.[9] Later in this chapter, I dive deeper into the ways that political bots, like other bots, are extensions of their builders' intentions—they are *political bot proxies*. Yes, bots can sometimes do unexpected things (although probably less often than you think), but in general, their code and the behavior it produces reflect the particular values of their creators. But before we turn to these larger claims, let's first look at who is creating political bots and why they are doing so.

Who Is the Automated Political Influencer?

Imagine what an automated political influencer looks like. Did you imagine a regular person—a neighbor, sports coach, grocery store clerk, accountant, or delivery driver? You probably didn't, but you should have. In the course of my research, I've talked to many very average-seeming people who hold down very average day jobs, but at home they run fairly complex computational propaganda campaigns on their own time. Most of them do so without any direction or support from a political campaign or government. They do it simply because they want to—because they believe in the causes and politics and viewpoints they are spreading, and they want to give them a wider currency. Of course, there are some individuals that receive some government support for this type of work; for example, citizens in Venezuela who spread pro-government Twitter propaganda receive small payments or vouchers from the state.[10] But this is not the case for the automated influencers I am interested in here. The people I am concerned with represent a phenomenon fairly singular to the present day: for the first time, technology now allows the "common man" (or, likely as not, the common woman) to run propaganda operations at scale without much coding knowledge or financial outlay. Easily available consumer-level technologies—the internet, various automation tools like "If This, Then That" (IFTTT), and increasingly approachable coding languages like Python (which my interviewees regularly mentioned as their go-to language for bot creation)—now allow propaganda to be created and spread by the mom next door, your father's fishing buddy, or that nice clerk at the hardware store.

D.W., a researcher and small business owner from the United Kingdom, told me that he used both social media bots and other forms of bots for a variety of purposes. He viewed his use of online automation as a form of political dissent, as activism. He first started "playing around" with bots when he became unemployed. In Britain, if you are unemployed you can receive a job seeker's allowance, but you must be actively applying for jobs. D.W. wrote a piece of code to automate job applications for him so that he could get his stipend. According to him, the terms and conditions of the government website did not prohibit automating the process, and to him this was a form of protest—an exercise that "expose[d] the horrible bureaucracy that people get caught up in for being poor." Later, he began building social media bots to spread messages of support for Jeremy Corbin and the U.K. Labour Party. D.W. experimented with different personalities for these political bots: some used humor, some were sincere, others were sarcastic or passive. His goal, he said, was to figure out which one got people to actually engage. He was after behavioral change.

While D.W. is a fairly typical automated political influencer, individual influencers can have different motivations. D.W. does most of what he does for political reasons, because he is *individually* invested in politics. Other individual automated political influencers work for money. These influencers are not being paid in the same way as the villagers in Venezuela—being paid cents on the dollar by the government for tweets. Many of the automated political influencers I spoke to in this category saw their bot-building as a freelance business. Many offered their services via websites like Fiverr, an Israeli-based online marketplace where people bid rock-bottom prices for online services; this subset of influencers sold or rented social media bots for small amounts of money. Other freelance bot builders used social media bots to bring in ad revenue by driving attention to their own social media profiles or websites. Still others had large, sophisticated operations, renting out entire social media botnets to anyone with money. A teammate at Oxford spoke to the proprietor of one such operation in Poland, who said he maintained over forty thousand unique online identities that he rented out for "guerilla marketing" purposes.[11] His accounts—cyborg accounts that used both automation and human oversight—could be launched to talk up particular products or companies in a way that seemed organic. As he openly admitted during the interview, he had also rented his accounts out for political purposes during national and European Union–wide electoral campaigns.

Most of these individual digital propagandists' bot accounts take advantage of online anonymity (although some—especially those seeking ad revenue—did automate social media profiles that used their real names). They all depend to some degree on bots, sock-puppets, or other automated features of the web, including trending and recommendation algorithms. And definitionally, the influencers I discuss here all engaged in at least some inherently political work. The influencers I sought out and spoke to are not those who use bots simply to sell regular commercial products (though some do that too): the people I am talking about here are all using digital tools to sell political ideas.

There has been a recent shift in how automated political influencers (and even organic, nonautomated political influencers) operate. Political campaigns and other elite actor groups have taken notice of influencers who are interested in politics—both celebrity and small-scale. Members of my research team and I documented our research in Wired into the rise of the latter group—what we called the partisan nanoinfluencer in politics.[12] These nanoinfluencers, who generally have a following of five thousand or fewer, are now being recruited *and paid* by political campaigns and other groups to spread particular types of content during elections. According to the digital political marketers we have spoken to, the logic is that these regular people have more intimate, local connections with their followers, and because of this their messages hit harder. (This is the same principle as previously discussed about the WhatsApp propaganda: that we are more likely to believe and act on information we hear from a trusted source with whom we feel a personal connection.) According to our own experience and that of other researchers, it's likely that some of these influencers—both celebrity influencers and "regular" nanoinfluencers—use social bots to achieve their goals.[13] In the rest of this chapter, I recount stories from these nanoinfluencers—

specifically, those noncelebrity social media users who have figured out how to use bots to amplify their opinions, whether for personal reasons or for money.

Automated Political Influencers Around the Globe

Remember Haluk, the political bot maker I spoke about in chapter 3—the one who worked *against* the Turkish government? He is a great example of an individual automated political influencer. He wasn't getting paid to do what he did. He had a regular day job and maintained his bots in his spare time. In our interview, he spoke about his opposition to Erdoğan's Justice and Development Party and about the fact that he built the bots on behalf of the People's Democratic Party. But the more I learned about his story, the more I realized that he was doing what he was doing for his own reasons.

For Haluk (as for D.W.), using political bots on social media was about leveling the playing field. As an IT professional with knowledge of software development, the Turkish builder was well positioned to undertake the task of launching bot accounts through the Twitter application programming interface (API). He, like D.W., seemed to believe that the bots weren't just amplifiers; they were time savers (and emotional energy savers). The automated accounts he built kept his friends and fellow People's Democratic Party members from having to actually engage with their adversaries to counteract the opposition's messaging. Instead, they could *automatically* respond to "Twitter bombs"—massive amounts of automated content dropped by the Turkish government into rival hashtag conversations. Turkey (like Syria) often used this Twitter bomb method against its own citizens in order to exhaust their opposition and frighten them into thinking they were fighting against a vast majority. These governments programmed bots to send thousands of junk tweets containing a given hashtag being used by their opposition. The tweets contained random images or quotes pulled from Google rather than actual vitriol or identifiable counterpropaganda; this helped the Twitter bombers evade detection. Their goal here was simply to introduce noise into the conversation—and to pollute the hashtag—in order to derail it. The Turkish bot builder's goal was to respond with the *illusion* of interaction to frustrate that goal.

Another automated digital influencer I interviewed, Azul, was a digital artist in the United States who built bots using IFTTT as a hobby. Azul used bots for a similar reason: to save time arguing with other users. She called her bots "dancing bear-ware." She told me that she cribbed the term from a book she had read titled *The Inmates Are Running the Asylum.*[14] The book, written in the late 1990s, centered the idea that much of the digital technology coming out worked, but not particularly well. As with a dancing bear, people just found it amazing that the given product sort of functioned. The premise of dancing bear bots is the same. They don't need to be technically great; they just need to do something unexpected to catch and keep people's attention—especially the attention of trolls on the opposite side of the political spectrum. The goal is to keep adversaries busy, or at the very least annoy them.

A fellow named Freeman, an expert on cybercrime and hacking based in Berlin, echoed Azul's point that bots needn't be very technically advanced or even particularly functional. He told me that bots don't need to be perfect to manipulate someone (or something, like another bot) into doing something. He said that a Twitter bot can tweet 50 percent gibberish and 50 percent sense and still be successful at driving people and/or other bots in the direction needed. Just like spam and phishing campaigns, he pointed out, bots can be successful without needing to communicate clearly, in real, convincingly human sentences. If people click on the links, they are on the hook.

Azul told me that her dancing bear-ware bots often tweeted on political issues in order to attract a particular clientele; they thus served to prevent political trolls on Twitter from harassing or attempting to start arguments with people. This allowed regular users to then use the platform as it "should" be used. For her, Twitter was not a venue for starting random arguments with people she didn't know (she joked that she saved that for Reddit). Rather, she saw Twitter as a platform of "brief engagement" with thoughts about the news and so on. If the dancing bear bots successfully took up the time of one troll, keeping that troll from focusing their attention on an actual person, she had achieved her purpose.

Angela, another hobbyist bot builder, echoed the utility of using bots to attract and occupy trolls, but she also spoke of the power of organized political bot networks that zeroed in on certain topics. According to her, these bots are honeypots that can be constructed to attract other bots programmed to seek out accounts talking about trends or other topics. She thinks of bots as both the worst and best of Twitter. According to her, bots engaged in vibrant work that encompassed comedy, journalism, and art, and these bots could make Twitter more approachable, fun, and democratic. As she said, "They can also be strangely poetic," recontextualizing the social media sphere and pushing boundaries. On the flip side, however, "manipulative bots make the platform difficult to use and the information there hard to parse," and they can be used for intense harassment, trolling women and journalists or attacking marginalized communities.

Other automated political influencers I spoke to used bots less for defense than for offense. Rather than building dancing bear-ware to keep political bots and trolls busy, they build their own bespoke networks of political bots to spread opinion, information, and disinformation on sites like Twitter and Facebook. Rick, a far-right automated political influencer, contacted me via my public university e-mail account because he noticed my colleagues and I had written about one of his Twitter accounts—I had described it as one of the most active political bots in the days preceding the 2016 U.S. election. He wanted to let me know that the account in question, along with the numerous others he ran, were not bots. They were real people—or, rather, he was a real person, and he ran them. In fact, after we talked, he changed the random names used on some of his Twitter accounts to his real name. Rick missed a fundamental point: there are always people behind bots. Automation simply extends a person's ability to communicate with people or interact with a system.

In many ways, Rick was like many other bot builders I've spoken to across the world. Uniquely, however, he was an out-and-out professional software developer. Unlike many of the other automated political influencers I interviewed, he used his coding skills in his day job. What he shared with the other builders was his motivation: he built his "software-enabled accounts" because he fervently believed in and wanted to spread a particular politics—in his case, hyper-conservative, right-wing politics. He would often step in and argue with people who spoke out against his bots' content. And he was prolific; he built and ran his own server, and he claimed that he often had as many as five computers running his accounts at a given time. A huge amount of the content Rick's accounts shared on Twitter was false and vitriolic information on highly partisan topics like immigration. My interview with Rick showed me something important: people like him can effectively use bots to control entire conversations on a platform like Twitter.

While most of the automated political influencers I have mentioned so far have worked primarily alone or with a few others who share the same views, some of these individual influencers do have support from more established, well-resourced groups, placing them in a gray area between these two broad types of computational propagandists. The Propaganda Research Lab, the team I lead within the University of Texas at Austin's Center for Media Engagement, has recently focused on interviewing people who leverage automation, disinformation, and other computational propaganda tools over encrypted chat apps and other closed messaging apps. Specifically, we've been speaking to people in India, Mexico, Brazil, and the United States. I've been particularly surprised by the interviews with political social media experts and members of so-called IT cells working on behalf of Modi's BJP in India (see chapter 2). They mention using bots as one tool for spreading political content on WhatsApp, the most popular space for the operations of Modi's "information warriors." While they do not rely only on bots (they also use a lot of human labor), the IT cell network in India has the hallmarks of individual automated political influencing combined with the support, resources, and strategies of state-based computational propagandists. I think of this group as "freelancers": not entirely volunteer yet not fully part of an official state-run digital propaganda machine like that in Turkey. Although one prominent BJP "IT cell" member adamantly claimed that he and those like him were volunteers, Modi and his BJP use both professional and volunteer labor, and other authoritarian leaders (Duterte in the Philippines, Bolsonaro in Brazil, and Trump in the United States) have followed suit.

What sets the BJP's network apart is its centralized, explicit training that teaches IT "yoddhas" or warriors the most effective digital propaganda techniques. These yoddhas return to their home villages, cities, and states, where they spread these skills to their neighbors in an "each one teach one" model. These local people can then help to spread pro-party and anti-opposition messages over WhatsApp. Because of this sort of pyramid scheme, it isn't clear where state-led propaganda activities end and individual ones begin. Some of the people running IT cells in India seem to be doing so of their own volition, without any access to party funds or directions. Others work fully within the party infrastructure. Still others are somewhere in between, taking general or indirect advice from people higher up the chain—including from Modi and his top advisers' own social media feeds—and using that as they see fit.

While access to bots and the tools of computational propaganda is being democratized, it is certainly not yet universal. Only certain people in certain places have the access and ability to build bots, especially without some sort of external support like that provided by the BJP. Most of the bot makers I talk about in this chapter— D.W., Azul, Rick, and Roger, discussed below—came from wealthy Western countries, and the Turkish bot builder had an advanced university degree. The internet's democratization of content production (including the production of computational propaganda) has primarily favored relatively well-to-do people in highly economically developed countries. In fact, it is another instance of the digital divide: computer skills (from basic use to advanced coding) are governed by access to education, money, infrastructure, and other sociocultural benefits that are only afforded to certain people.

The Bot Proxy

My work with bot makers and digital propagandists asks some key questions that can help us understand the global system of automated political influence: How do less-resourced individuals and groups of citizens use automation over social media for the purposes of political communication? Who are these individuals, and what are their goals? What does today's bottom-up (rather than top-down) organization of propaganda dissemination mean for current understandings of digital disinformation?

In March 2016, I made a trip to Detroit, Michigan, to do field-work around the presidential primary in that state. My main goal was to establish contact with people working directly for the various campaigns in order to understand whether—and if so, how—campaigns were making use of social bots in their digital marketing efforts. On the day before the primary, I was standing in line for a Clinton rally at the Museum of African American History. During the wait, I had a conversation with a small group of Michigan State students. We discussed our reasons for attending, and I told them about my research on political bots and the U.S. election. It turned out that a couple of the students had more than a cursory understanding of social media bots being used in politics. In fact, they told me they had peers who had used social bots over Twitter to spread political news. The next day, while volunteering in one of the Clinton campaign's Get Out the Vote call centers, another informant told me they had a friend who was using social bots on the dating app Tinder to spread information to her romantic matches about why they should vote for Bernie Sanders.

The people building these bots were not working, or even volunteering, for campaigns. They were simply using their knowledge of bots and coding to facilitate their ability to engage in politics, using automation to amplify their reach. This was at a time when nobody was talking about bots or disinformation ("fake news"). Indeed, in the months that followed, I often had to explain to security experts and computer scientists what I meant when I talked about the use of socially oriented bots in online political communication—in other words, when I talked about the simple, accessible, highly democratized technologies that people were already using to spread propaganda. The problem was that most of the experts I spoke to knew *too much* about bot use. Their conceptions were highly technologically sophisticated, bound up in the broader use of autonomous soft-ware—web scrapers, spiders, crawlers—or in the virally infected computers (known as "bots") that are used for direct denial of ser-vice attacks. They were not thinking about the democratization of access to coding and bot-creation tools (or the wealth of freely avail-able YouTube tutorials). The bots these experts were making and thinking about are not the kinds of simple political bots and tools that college students use to communicate ideas with their extended networks in their everyday lives. Most of my informants, like Rick from earlier in this chapter, built simple bots to engage in poli-tics, using this and other digital tools as a means to particular ends that reflected their values. These bots were political proxies for their creators.

Many social media users talk about popular public-facing bots like @OliviaTaters or Xiaoice as if they were automatons who think—as one interviewee put it, as if they were Star Wars characters: like C-3PO with his human-like artificial intelligence, or like R2-D2, the eccentric robot helper with his charming bleeps and bloops. But bots are not social beings; they are not their creators. While creators often give their bots human names and creative personalities, speak-ing about them like friends or pets, social bots are fundamentally built to do tasks *specified by developers*. Most bots on social media are semi-automated tools that allow the person who launches them to interact with platforms both on the back end, communicating with servers, applications, and databases, and on the front end, interacting with human users.

Harry was one of the first builders to articulate the complex re-lationship between the bot and its builder. Referencing the work of Ian Bogost, he said, "Bots are independent objects that do the work of the philosopher."[15] This is a concept that requires some unpack-ing. First, Harry wanted to make it clear that bots are separate from their creators—they function autonomously. Second, he saw the philosopher-builder as someone who builds particular functions into these digital objects and then relinquishes the majority of control over their activities in the world. Yes, bots do the work of the person that constructs and releases them (even bots such as Microsoft's @Tay, which was built with advanced machine learning to interact with Twitter users, reflect the imperfections and biases of their builders), but they also have their own identities and interact with the internet in ways that are independent from that builder. After many discussions with those who build and launch social bots on social media platforms, we have come to see bots as extensions of their creators—neither fully separate from nor fully coextensive with the people who build them.

Perhaps the most interesting way in which they act for (and like) their creators is this: bots, like their human creators, enact change on systems that change them in return. Bots that interact with complex social systems have the ability to do things beyond the expectations of their builders—to achieve the unexpected. A bot stands in for, and often carries out, the will of the person who built it, but a bot can also challenge the authority of its maker. It functions and interacts with its environment both automatically and independently. Bots thus reflect both the builder *and* the networked computational systems in which they operate.

As my colleagues and I argue in a previous paper on this subject, people who build bots do so with particular intentions.[16] Some builders, like Azul, intend to get other users' attention and keep them busy. Others, like D.W. and Rick, intend to spread their own particular political views or to game computational systems. At times, however, the designer intentions that a given bot is built to carry out can be muddled as the bot interacts with the broader ecosystem in which it operates. On social media platforms, a diverse range of inputs and outputs from other people or programs can affect the bot's actions, and it is hard to predict exactly how any social program will function under different stresses. For instance, bots designed to get attention can get too much attention. One experimental bot builder who programmed his bot to learn from its surroundings woke up one day to find the police at his door: his bot had unexpectedly started threatening to kill people.[17] Instead of gaming the system, the system (likely other users) gamed the bot. This is what I mean when I say the bot is a proxy for its creator—not a perfect representational mirror of its builder but a separate entity.

Walter, an out-of-work artist and amateur bot builder from Israel, told me about his sense that the bots he made were enacting his values in the world. Walter (who said that he was not a great coder but that "new tools like Cheap Bots, Done Quick and Tracery have helped [him] to make functioning social bots") told me that he found catharsis in building bots that argued with trolls and bullies on the opposite side of the political spectrum from him. He felt like he was doing something useful—engaging in activism—by keeping potential trolls engaged with automated accounts, but by using bots to do the debating for him, he preserved his own emotional well-being. Walter's bots, like Azul's, were specifically built to argue with subsets of people who held particular views (identified by automated keyword searches) or who were using specific hashtags. In other words, Walter's bots were encoded with his values and designed to enact them in the world. Similarly, Roger, a retiree who builds political bots in his spare time, explained to me that bots are tools a person uses to convey particular intentions. They are not in themselves good or evil, politically motivated or not. According to Roger, the creator's intention is crucial: for example, he said that it was as easy for him to make bots that brought people together over an issue as to make bots that divided them.

My interviewees have consistently articulated the proxy relationship I describe here, placing themselves as separate from but related to, or invested in, the bots they build. Bots thus challenge the rigid separation between humans and technologies, makers and mediums. When social and political bots act for their builders, they encode their builders' intentions and values, extending them into the world by enacting them in interactions with other users. Bots are a threshold, an interface between human and machine: they are programmed by their creators (a human-to-computer interaction), and they do their work in their interactions with other users (a computer-to-human interaction). Therefore, bots not only reveal information about their creators' values, intentions, and desires; they also reveal, exploit, and change aspects of the platforms and digital systems that make them possible.

Technical Infrastructure

Because of these bot-system interactions, it is too simplistic to say that automation on sites like Twitter or Facebook is purely functional or instrumental. It is more accurate to say that the technical infrastructure of the hosting platform constrains and shapes how bots can function. For example, the degree of back-end accessibility the platform allows—the application programming interface (API)—affects how, or whether, bots built by outside developers can function on the site at all. The API is a request and response mechanism for exchanging data with the remote servers where all large online sites store their information. Some companies make some APIs public to grant access to particular data from the site. One Twitter API, for example, gives researchers access to 1 percent of Twitter data on a given subject—a representative sample, according to the company. Other APIs allow coders to actively launch software programs.

The platform infrastructure also governs how social networking occurs on the site, which itself has a large effect on how successfully bots can function. The political bot makers I spoke to told me that Twitter was their platform of choice because of its particular construction and the social network it produced. For similar infrastructural reasons, many successfully launched political bots on Reddit, Tumblr, and Tinder. Harry put it this way: "Different platforms, and different communities, have different technical and social benefits for bots." Harry explained why certain sites are more difficult for bot makers to use: Facebook and Instagram, for example, make it challenging to launch successful social bots because Facebook's API and algorithms are always changing, and Instagram does not allow photos (the central focus of the site) to be posted through its API.

That said, several other builders told me about, and were even able to show me, successful Facebook bots. One builder broke down Facebook bots by function: messenger bots, bots for data collection, and bots that imitate human users. The Facebook bot builders launched their bots through Facebook's Graph API or browser emulation, with the latter proving most successful in launching small-scale bots that imitated regular profiles. Many builders also told me that they deployed bots to automate political event and group pages. Automated pages seem acceptable to Facebook; two different builders told me that when Facebook caught their fake automated human profiles, the company told them to create an automated page rather than forcing them to delete the bot.

Platform infrastructure does not only dictate how easy it is to design bots for the platform; it also dictates the different "shapes" of user networks, and therefore the different "shapes" of users' interactions with other users. Different social platforms foster different interactions, and this affects how, or whether, bots can work to drive political communication on the site. On Facebook, for example, users tend to communicate with friends and family or with people who are directly connected to those friends and family. It is relatively uncommon to follow or interact with people with whom you have no real-life ties. On Twitter, however, most users interact with a much broader variety of other users: some friends and family, perhaps, but also journalists, politicians, professional athletes, and, yes, random users. Twitter's greater network flexibility means socially oriented bots are more likely to successfully interact with, and even change the opinions of, people using the site.

While Facebook's APIs have always been relatively limited and inaccessible, Twitter's have always been fairly open—a decision originally intended to democratize access for creative users schooled in coding. This means that developers can interact with Twitter and its data in all sorts of ways beyond the manicured front-end pages that greet noncoding users. They can write code to streamline their own experience or launch software to make the site better for other users. Twitter's open API allows users to write software that automatically creates and posts content, or that automatically likes, retweets, or interacts with posts from other users. This software is a Twitter bot.

In a twist that should not surprise you, Twitter's open API access, originally meant to facilitate democratic innovation on the site, is now being exploited by coders to spread computational propaganda. Some of these bot builders are, as previously mentioned, paid campaigners: political groups employ people with sophisticated coding knowledge to launch armies of bots that automatically stump for their candidate. According to Jam, an accountant who builds bots to unofficially support political parties, these political bots are modern versions of the claque—the age-old tradition of political candidates planting supporters in the crowd. This is not a bad comparison; bots, like supporters hiding in a not-yet-committed crowd, can make the candidate and his ideas look much more popular than they are—can nudge others to jump on the bandwagon.

Making Money Versus Making a Statement

Automated political influencers have two broad, sometimes intertwining motivations for launching political bots and sockpuppet accounts: profit and persuasion. First, some of these actors use these tools to make money. There are several well-documented cases of bot makers doing this. For example, Jestin Coler, the person behind the false news sites the National Report and the Denver Guardian, has spoken publicly about using social media posts to drive users to his sites for ad revenue. According to Coler, some articles garnered as many as 8 million views, and "with each click, he made money on ads—over $10,000 a month."[18]

The second motivation for bot makers is to spread their opinions and to influence other people to change their beliefs or behaviors. In my interview with Roger, he told me that people like Coler often use bots to "plant and boost conversations about particular topics." I regularly saw evidence that people used bots in order to post more messages, thus publicizing their political opinions more widely. All of the bot makers discussed above are evidence of this. These users' bots seek to make a point rather than make money. Many partisan-motivated influencers use their profiles to (unwittingly) market fake news, believing that they are doing altruistic work to help their country. These bot builders often (rather defensively) pointed out that their activities were not breaking any rules. When I asked about the ethics of deploying his own opinions at scale using bots, one amateur bot builder from Illinois said that he was not breaking any of Twitter's terms of service—indeed, that he was following them to the letter. He said he was using the site precisely as it was designed to be used, because bots have always had a place there.

The two motivations cannot always be separated. Conversations with informants, reports in news stories, and my own observations of bots on social media show over and over again that while some bot makers will spread any political idea for money, and some will spread their own political ideas for free, many do both: they spread their own particular political ideas, using both social automation and human networking, in order to make money. In other words, money-seeking bot makers' beliefs often coincided with the political bots that they were building and launching. Not always, though; in some rare circumstances—such as the 2016 U.S. presidential election—money-seeking makers are purely mercenary and will deploy bots on the side of whoever pays them. These bot makers may even reside in a different country and electoral system from the one they are messaging about.

Perhaps the most interesting, and the most dangerous, type of political bot is the "cyborg" type—the account that is half-bot, half-human. In late 2016, I came across information suggesting that small groups of users had begun deploying covert social cyborg (semi-automated) accounts, which were at some times run by bots and at other times run by people. They used these accounts to seed political ideas or links to "fake news" websites among groups of unwitting human users, who then spread this information seemingly organically, in Facebook groups thousands strong.

According to someone I call Mayer, a computational researcher who claimed to have tested similar techniques, these tactics worked best on Facebook group pages because (unlike the usual Facebook networks, which connect people with real-life ties) people in Facebook groups are usually connecting with people they do not know.

According to Mayer, these "cyborg armies" were effective in beginning conversations because people didn't expect automation—let alone the more nuanced communications possible with cyborg accounts—on Facebook group pages. (Twitter users are more alert to this possibility because nearly everyone now knows that Twitter is hospitable to bots.) As mentioned earlier, Facebook group pages are much more forgiving about automation and anonymity than personal pages. The engineers of these cyborg bot efforts used this loophole, as well as the hybrid nature of the cyborg bots, to evade both the algorithmic bot detectors and the human oversight that are intended to detect automated behavior and the gaming of trends. The hybridity of these accounts likely allowed them to evade some of the controls on bot activity. For example, with some degree of human involvement, these accounts could log in through the front end of the platform instead of the back end to which bots are normally relegated. In addition, these cyborg accounts were much subtler in their approach, only seeding their ideas to be picked up and spread by others, rather than force-spreading them by obvious spamming. Once these accounts' ideas were picked up by regular users on group pages, the cyborg accounts faded out of the conversation or were deleted outright. These tactics allowed political ideas to spread in a way that seemed more natural, and these accounts were less often flagged by site administrators. Their ability to imitate grassroots spread meant that they successfully drove regular users to linked sites, increasing advertising revenue for the original architects.[19]

Anonymity Versus Transparency?

Unlike the people discussed above, some automated political influencers who sought to change opinion and behavior were entirely transparent about the fact their bots were automated. Pan, an educator living in Chicago, spoke to me about just such a bot, which he said he had built as a form of social commentary. This particular Twitter bot used automation to scrape information from an open database of facts about nuclear arms and disarmament and post statistics to Twitter. Pan's hope was that the bot would draw attention to the problem of nuclear arms and cause people to think about it more deeply. Pan's bot has over fifty thousand followers and has been written about in major news media.

Pan calls his interest in bot-making an "avocation [hobby] rather than a vocation." Although he does not use his bots to spread inflammatory news stories or make money, he is a prime example of an automated political influencer. Like other computational propaganda bots, his seek to make political provocations and change user opinions and behaviors; operate beyond the capacity of a human user (although they are usually singular, not mutually supportive networks of interrelated botnets); and seek to spread information (though his bots spread established facts rather than disinformation or defamatory posts). How, then, do his bots differ from amplification or political harassment bots?

First, Pan builds his bots to be transparent about being bots. Many political bots are deceptive, attempting to trick human users into believing they are human. Second, deceptive bots often spread biased or factually inaccurate information while Pan's traffic in established facts accessed from accurate, credible online databases (often from libraries or museums). Third, Pan's bots work to make political discourse richer rather than to interrupt, misdirect, or muddle it.

Useful bots (like Pan's) do exist on social media. Bots are simply tools for finding, parsing, and spreading information; it is how and why they are used that really matters in the context of political communication. This is why calls to ban all bots on sites like Twitter miss the mark: they place the blame on the tool (which is not in itself inherently bad) rather than on the creator that designed and deployed it. Because bots are proxies for their creators, it is the creator's motivations and intentions that make bots either useful or damaging. In Pan's words, "Because bots only do what people tell them do, they also come with all of the bias of their creator." When bots are not transparent about their status as bots, they occlude their creators' motivations: Pan noted that "the bias of a bot is hidden by the way people interact with the bot on a site like Twitter." As he observed, the "mechanical" bot provides a layer of obfuscation between the builder and other platform users: "The bot gives the coder a bit of distance from the content that shows up on someone's screen. People can't see what is going on behind the scenes, so to speak." He further emphasized the sense that the bot's distance from the creator serves as a shield for the bot maker, saying, "If I, or a team of people, was manually tweeting this content other users would expect a quick human response when they asked questions or spoke to the account. They would hold us accountable. It is harder, though, to ascribe intentions to a bot than it is to a human." In other words, although you can attribute much of a bot's design and behavior to its creator, users recognize that the two are not identical. After all, bots can be changed by a given system even as they change it.

But what does this mean for accountability? Who is responsible for the bot's actions—and the consequences of those actions? For example, who is responsible when a bot programmed to learn from its surroundings does or says something unexpected, as did the bot who threatened murder? What about the millions of human users being targeted by bots—do they have a right to privacy from bots? What is the responsibility of bots and their creators for the noisy system they create, particularly if this automated noise slows or halts the democratic process? As I go to press with this book, we are in the middle of a digital spin campaign aimed at muddying the results of the 2020 U.S. election. I've been tracking swaths of automated and sockpuppet social media accounts spreading disinformation about Joe Biden "stealing the election" and false accounts of vote counters manipulating ballot results in swing states. Who is responsible for what occurs—directly or indirectly—because of this digital deception? Who is to blame if, say, people try to kidnap a governor or if they show up to elected officials' homes to harass them or if they storm the Capitol because of what they've seen online? Of course, the people who actually engage in these hypothetical offline activities are responsible for their own actions, but what about those that purposefully provoke them to such ends?

5

Social Media Companies, the Technology Industry, and Propaganda

In the fall of 2020, just two months before the U.S. presidential election, several members of my research team and I sat down for an interview with Dev, a high-level ex-employee of a social media company. The former software engineer and executive was blunt in his assessment of his former employer and its competitors: "These are not social media companies, these are advertising companies." What he meant, he explained, was that they benefit from virality, whether it stems from a conspiratorial political meme or a corporate ad campaign; they make money from the spread of content, whether the content is good or bad, true or false, useful or damaging. The more we talked to Dev, the clearer it became that he believed the current major social media companies would never truly address the problems of computational propaganda and disinformation—or at least would not do so systematically. Instead, he said, they will simply keep chipping away here and there in order to give the illusion of progress, all while continuing to rake in money from ads, data sales, and other ventures premised on users' attention and behavior.

According to Dev, there isn't much about users that social media companies don't track and profit from. Firms ascribe particular "engagement" values, in stacked order, to nearly every user action that occurs on their apps or sites: comments, likes, views, and so on. Each of these user actions represents a level of engagement. The more interaction/engagement the content gets, the more the social media firm can charge for it. Facebook, Twitter, YouTube, and others compete to sell user interaction to the highest bidder. As experts have pointed out, this is a profit system, grounded in the principle that more active users and groups are more likely to consume ads. When they do consume ads, the companies who place the ads pay the platform for those views and clicks. In addition, information about the ads that users consume is collected through surveillance, and this information produces better user behavioral data, which can also be sold.[1] Attention is a commodity, and social media platforms are human-designed systems that leverage computational power to get and keep people's attention on a range of issues—to profit from altering the ways users act and interact.[2]

Like bots, social media platforms are strings of code and algorithms designed to create behavioral change. And like bots, the computational mechanisms that make up the substrate of social media—the software and hardware that make it all work—are not sentient beings but a combination of mathematics and machinery which also encode the values and biases of their creators. And again like bots, these tools are altered via society and sociological forces—ideas that have been explored by science and technology studies (STS) for years.[3]

Like bots, then, social media platforms are proxies for their creators. Yet folks in Silicon Valley, from Mark Zuckerberg to Jack Dorsey, work hard to evade responsibility for what their tools, particularly social media, do.[4] There are two primary aspects of computational systems and the internet that these creators use to occlude any responsibility for the effects of the platforms they created. The first is complexity. Because most people don't understand computer science (and most that do are denied access to Facebook's or Twitter's core algorithms), tech leaders have constantly been able to shuck their responsibility onto obscure mathematic processes. They often try to frame these processes as "objective," ignoring the critical ways that human people affect the things they make.[5] The second is the individualization of responsibility for the problems of social media. Firms do not take responsibility for problems such as computational propaganda; they dump it on users. Because their algorithms are supposedly "objective," disinformation and propaganda must be a "user problem." According to the companies, it is not the fault of the technologists—or the apps and sites they build—if manipulative content is spread on them. It is the fault of propagandists. "We are a technology platform," they argue, "not a media company." But as anyone with common sense can see, the responsibility is shared: it is the fault of companies and their products *and* of those working to spread divisive political content on their systems. The companies make decisions that allow propaganda to thrive on social media, in part because, as I explained, *user engagement and viral content create profit.*

Dev drove this point home again and again. He told us that the goal of a democratic government—to protect the people—is diametrically opposed to the ruling goal of social media companies: to protect the bottom line. "When you look at the value chain," he said, "it's not a good story for societies in general." The Zuckerbergs and Dorseys of the world tout their platforms as ideal mechanisms for civil discourse, but according to Dev, they have it completely backwards. The ancient premise that democracy is born from open debate and discussion does not hold when there are literal intermediations interposed between people. "You've seen road rage," he said. "When you're in a big hunk of metal separated from everyone you are a lot more likely to behave badly than [when] you are face to face." He argues that this is especially true when the intermediating mechanism—here, social media—is purpose-built to hook your emotions and retain your attention. In the end, Dev argued, the systems as designed lead people to treat one another as objects. The world is unlikely to be changed for the better by people rage-messaging at one another online.

The systematic problems of social media—both the human biases encoded into the algorithms and the baked-in predation on which the whole idea is premised—have produced the computational propaganda landscape we have today.[6,7] The ability to manufacture consensus is built on the idea that when other people value something (here, expressed by viewing, liking, commenting on, and trending certain ideas), we are more likely to value it also. This is precisely the behavior that social media is designed to foster. And the bot makers take advantage of this. According to Dev, "Many of the people building and launching [political bot and sockpuppet] accounts are mercenaries." They are freeloaders hired to do one thing—operate a persona on behalf of a political group—but are actually totally focused on selling something else to benefit themselves.

Dev left our call with powerful parting words: "This is what we are dealing with, the commodification of influence apparatus. It's the simple truth:" Before the meteoric rise of today's social media platforms, bot and sockpuppet accounts were already being used by governments to manipulate public opinion online. But now social media has democratized content production, giving everyone the tools to easily get their ideas online. During the same period, the technical barriers to bot-making and automation have been drastically eroded: computing power in consumer-level electronics has increased exponentially (a computer in every pocket! It's like something out of *Star Trek*). And because of social media's profit model, there has been a dizzying increase in the level of interconnection between systems (much of it due to Amazon's AWS, the largest cloud platform on the planet, used by many social media websites) that track and store user data and behavioral information. Many of these systems are scrapable, meaning that user data is available to political influencers to aid in targeting ads or disinformation campaigns. It's a perfect storm for do-it-yourself propaganda-making.

Computational Propaganda Is Still Human Propaganda

In late 2017, I took a job at the Institute for the Future in Palo Alto, California.[8] The institute has been in the business of futures thinking for over fifty years now. A spinoff from RAND Corp, the think-tank/foresight incubator helps NGOs, companies, and governments around the world envision what might come next for them. For instance, in a collaborative report with Google News Labs, my colleagues and I helped the tech firm understand the reasons behind the growth of chat app usage among journalists in the Asia Pacific region.[9] We then leveraged these insights to discuss the implications for how platforms like Signal, WhatsApp, WeChat, and Telegram might affect news-making in years to come.

The institute hired me to start the Digital Intelligence Lab, a social scientific research entity aimed at analyzing how emerging technologies were being used to both enable and restrict democratic communication. My goal with the lab was to continue the work I'd done at Oxford on computational propaganda but to expand it to focus on questions related to political speech and artificial intelligence, virtual reality, and other novel technologies. The best representation of this work can be found in my book *The Reality Game,* which outlines how these emerging tools and techniques are already being employed in attempts to control the flow of communication around the world.[10] *The Reality Game* also outlines ways that society can respond by building more socially conscious technical systems—what I call "designing with human rights in mind."

One of the best parts about working at the institute was that it put me right in the middle of conversations with people from some of the most advanced technology companies in the world. Groups from various tech accelerators, cutting-edge startups, and massive tech firms regularly convened at the institute's office in downtown Palo Alto. The conversations that occurred during those meeting were unique, for they brought together the experiences and expertise of these tech folks with those of people from all sorts of other professions: academia, journalism, law, the nonprofit world, design, and so on. This produced wide-ranging conversations that did not center on technology but placed it into the broader social contexts in which it lives. These conversations humanized global society's biggest problems—including those playing out in our informational systems and social media platforms.

In the rarefied halls of the University of Oxford, it was easy for me to flatly criticize how tech firms were dealing with computational propaganda and manufactured consensus. But at the institute, when I actually met and talked to the people building those tools or doing user-experience work, my view of the situation became more complicated. I still believe that tech companies, especially social media companies, have a lot to answer for. Now, though, I understand three principles that I didn't before. These three principles are central to this chapter.

First, the beliefs and values of the people building technology are encoded into the tools they construct. Meeting the folks who design, launch, and maintain social media helped me to more tangibly understand their products because they were shaped by these individuals' values. Second, despite the intentions of the well-meaning technologists I met, there are always users—people who social media companies see as adversaries—on the other side, working to hack, game, and manipulate the tools and systems the moment they are launched. Third—and this precept grows out of the first two—social media platforms are exactly as flawed and as political as the people that create and use them. Trending and recommendation algorithms, as many fantastic researchers have pointed out, are neither organic nor objective.[11]

Culpable as the system is, though, it is not the only factor in the spread of computational propaganda. What we see transpiring on social media—from the rampant spread of disinformation to arguments borne out of serious political polarization, racism, and hate—is equally a result of the people behind the keyboards. Computational propaganda is still human propaganda. I do not mean to excuse the social media firms with this assertion. While working at the institute, I saw that Silicon Valley is no less complicit in the flow of propaganda than the mass media firms that came before—and continue to surround—it. In fact, these technology firms are a core part of the human and technological infrastructure that allows for manufactured consensus to continue. This is made clear in the quantitative work of Yochai Benkler and colleagues and the Computational Propaganda Project at Oxford, who observe that both "networked" and "computational" propaganda exist as part of a larger maelstrom of manipulated and manipulative information flowing from various groups to social media and from there to traditional media.[12] Using computational and network analyses, these groups have tracked the interplay between the various actors and sectors within the communication system. My ethnographic work in Silicon Valley has made this even more palpable for me. As I've navigated back and forth between industry folks and academics, between bot makers and bot trackers, and between propagandists and journalists, I've come to deeply feel the connections among them all. Like the mass media organizations laid bare by Edward Herman and Noam

Chomsky, all of these groups are entrenched within our political-economic system and are therefore involved in perpetuating systems of power—in propaganda.[13]

The Beliefs of Social Media Firm Employees

In the previous chapter, I explained that bots are proxies for their creators—extensions of the people who build them. This is equally true for the most sophisticated machine learning social bots, built to learn from their environment. Indeed, this claim is simply a microversion of a larger truth: because technology is built by people, it contains their values, desires, and biases, and it is informed by the larger culture and society within which it is constructed and intended to operate.[14]

With this in mind, we can see how particular types of propaganda quickly gained the upper hand online. If a racist person builds a news recommendation algorithm for a social media website or application, it is very much possible that algorithm will prioritize racist content for users.[15] Similarly, if someone on the far left or far right of the political spectrum is the project manager for a software system built to detect disinformation, they might weed out more websites and content that do not agree with their politics. This can happen either consciously or subconsciously. There are very real examples of people intentionally building biased and propagandistic social media features; there are probably even more examples of designers and engineers unintentionally creating online tools that manufacture the illusion of consensus.[16,17] We will likely never know whether the hordes of Twitter engineers who designed the platform meant to allow social bots to amplify certain types of content, including political content, for tech encodes latent bias just as well as it does explicit bias. When an image auto-crop mechanism more readily focuses on white faces, for instance, it's more likely to be from the unconscious biases of a given coder or coders than from the machinations of overt white nationalists seeking to discriminate.

My own research has again and again revealed how technologists and engineers' biases make possible (or worsen) the spread of computational propaganda. In the fall of 2018, I had one of many conversations at a coffee shop with a social media firm employee named Danny. Danny worked on the policy side of social media, but he claimed to have a decent understanding of the technology too. The executives of the company he worked for publicly stated on their standard employment application that their platform was not infested with bots—a claim that was contradicted by my research and that of many colleagues. Several times during our conversation, Danny parroted the company's view, saying things like "political bots aren't really an issue for us." I asked him why he thought this. He said that it was partly because users were required to use their real names but primarily because (unlike Twitter) his company's social media site didn't give people the ability to launch bots through their application programming interface (API)—which, he kept telling me, was the cause of Twitter's bot problems.

What I'd seen online and heard in my offline fieldwork made me push Danny about this belief. "Have you heard of headless browsing?" I asked him. He hadn't. "Well," I explained, "I recently had a meeting with a coder who showed me precisely how possible it was to use this technique in order to leverage political bots on your app without ever having to use the API." *Headless browsing* is a technique that involves building a software tool with automated control over a given web page in a way similar to how a person would experience it through, say, Safari or Firefox. "In this case," I said, "the bot can login to your app from the main access portal like human users." This meant that if Danny's colleagues were trying to detect bots by tracking particular features of API access, they wouldn't catch the account.

It's possible (even likely) that Danny's colleagues tasked with detecting fake traffic on the app were well aware of the problems posed by headless browsing. They might have even created a way to stop bots from accessing their app through that system. But how many people were tasked with working on bot detection, given that the entire company took the line that bots were not a problem for them? At an event weeks before, Danny's colleagues had claimed—in front of people from government and several other sectors—that manipulative bots and sockpuppet accounts were not a problem on their platform. At the same time, lead executives at his firm were saying the same thing in the national and international media. And Danny was following the company line. Because Danny and his coworkers staunchly believed that bots weren't a problem on their platform, the company was failing to pay attention to a very real problem on the app—something I'd just seen in action days before. In fact, the policy team at this firm was actively, publicly denying that political bots were a problem to precisely those people trying to share insights that could help to fix the issue. Although Danny wasn't a developer and hadn't built any aspects of the social media site, it was clear to me that employees' beliefs about their firms show up in infrastructure; the weakness in the platform exploited by headless browsing would continue to exist because of employees' and leaders' beliefs.

I saw many other examples of how the beliefs developers engrain in their tools can allow computational propaganda to persist. One evening that same fall, I was invited to a dinner in Atherton, an especially wealthy little town in the valley. The dinner was intimate, with only ten or so people in attendance. I'd been invited by a friend who lived in a San Francisco co-op filled with people who worked at high-flying tech companies. One of the people at the party, Lukas, told me that he had been an early employee at one of the major social media companies. His job at the firm took several twists and turns but mostly he had worked on their recommendation algorithms. Obviously, I was intrigued; I knew that recommendation algorithms were one of the key ways makers of these sites "curated" information for their users. The people who wrote the code for recommendation algorithms were making key decisions about, for instance, what types of news a person was shown. (This curation is where their technology most clearly overlaps with the function of news media, which makes the same kinds of choices about what news to feature and what to bury.)

Because Lukas no longer worked at the firm, he was much more willing to talk to me than folks that still had jobs there, and it turned out Lukas was interested in topics related to my research. As I told him about what I studied, he peppered me with his own experiences and thoughts. "Look," I leveled with him, "do you think your own opinions and ideas affected how you and your team built the recommendation algorithms?" He guffawed. "Of course," he said. "How couldn't they?" He told me that over the years, the site had changed its focus from simple interpersonal interactions to information, news, and trends, making the recommendation algorithms more central to the site's operation. He also pointed out that by now, years after he'd worked there, hundreds if not thousands of different engineers had added their own stamps on the code that informed various recommendation algorithms. "It would be impossible to unravel how much bias has been built into the code at this point," he said. The code no longer reflected a few developers' biases but those of thousands of people with thousands of different viewpoints.

What might this mean for computational propaganda? First, the convoluted nature of the code—layers on layers of loophole-filling, bug-crushing, and feature-changing accreted atop the original base code—would make it difficult to determine how, or whether, particular political biases were built into it. These differing viewpoints might pull in opposite directions; for instance, the code might at the same time both regularly recommend conspiracy videos to users and have a bias toward suggesting left-wing media outlets. It would take a lot of work to pick apart the different layers of code causing these different biases. Second, the recommendation algorithm code, made of layers and layers of patches and changes, is infrastructural, meaning that many other portions of the site (each with its own layers of code, touched by hundreds of developers) has been built on top of it. Like a Jenga game, the whole structure would collapse if you pulled the recommendation coding to try to analyze bias and clean it up. According to Lukas, much of the code he and his team-mates had written was integral to not only how the site *functioned* but what the site *was*. Without it, the product would look completely different. Finally, Lukas made it clear that the original coders hadn't thought about how bots might be used to cause the algorithm to shift its recommendations. The site was built before bots were a twinkle in a politician's eye—in fact, political bots couldn't have been on anyone's mind because they developed in response to the ways that this site (and other social media sites) were built. Lukas and the other developers had built their algorithms on the assumption that if lots of users were looking at particular content, in must be popular, and the most popular content should be pushed to other users. This fundamental assumption ended up making it possible for future bot makers to launch thousands of bot accounts in order to game the algorithm for their own political goals.

Users Game the Tools Social Media Firms Build

My conversation with Lukas, particularly our discussion of the implications of algorithm construction, crystallized for me an idea that had come up in many other conversations I'd had. Specifically, Lukas's admission that he and his colleagues hadn't thought about bots or manipulation at all when doing their early work on the recommendation algorithm brought to mind two other discussions I'd had with political bot makers. The first was with a bot builder named Mercer; we had talked about the concept of building bots to talk to people versus building bots to talk to other code frameworks. The second, with a former Japanese journalist and bot enthusiast named Midori, focused on a story about how news outlets hired marketing firms to spread their articles on social media. Both conversations centered around the idea that social media recommendation algorithms were susceptible to manipulation or gaming through sheer numbers.

For the first year or so that I studied bots, I was hung up on the idea that people were building political bots to directly interact with other people on social media sites for various purposes. The bots I'd seen and heard about would do one of a couple of things on the front end of the platform. Some were built to try to engage people in arguments about certain political topics, either in order to actually change their minds or to simply waste their time. Others were used to spam hashtags associated with a particular political conversation in an attempt to drown out useful information, making searches for content using that hashtag pointless. Still other bots were designed to harass a particular journalist to stop them from reporting on a story—or silence them, full stop.

Mercer was the first bot builder to correct my mistake. He explained that bots weren't just built to communicate with other users—people or other bots—on social media. They weren't designed to affect political conversation only through front-end communication. Instead, many of the bots he built were intended to communicate directly with trending and recommendation algorithms. That is, they were built to "talk" to the code behind the front-facing platform via the back end of the site, through the API. "Why would I focus on trying to change someone's mind with a bot barely capable of communication," he said, "when I could get the trending algorithm on a site to reprioritize and reshare the content I'm pushing with five thousand bots?"

He used automated social media profiles to fake organic discussions of a given topic (for him, usually something to do with U.K. politics). The social media sites' code that identified popular content might then pick up on those conversations based on the sheer amount of chat on the topic, noting that topic as trending on its sidebar or home page for millions of users. Those users would think lots of others were discussing it, and might even click on it themselves, further driving the algorithm to push that content. Mercer, and several other bot builders and experts I spoke to later, all made a point of saying that these trends did not affect only individual users' preferences and behavior, as many news companies use trends in their reporting. Bot builders dream of getting their pet ideas into the mainstream media—a dream that Mercer claimed to have fulfilled with his bots.

This same idea of getting bot-driven ideas into mainstream media also featured in my conversation with Midori, but the who and the how differed. Midori had worked for a number of journalism websites of various sizes and calibers. Some of them, she explained, were struggling to figure out how to get their content to spread on social media. They hired marketing firms that claimed they could help news sites to "grow their audience" and get more clicks—thereby also getting more advertising money, now the sole source of revenue for many media organizations. Midori was a bot builder herself in her spare time, mostly creating bots for her own amusement and that of a small cadre of fans, and she noticed something strange about the tactics of one of these marketing companies. She thought they were using bots to share particular news articles from the outlet where she was working at the time. Basically, the bots—most of which she said were pretty unsophisticated, many of which lacked even profile pictures on their fake accounts—shared the same link to the article over and over and over. Midori thought the goal was twofold. First, other bots and even some human users would pick up on the story the bot had shared, resharing it themselves. Second, the algorithm on the social media site would relist the article as trending. This cycle stuck with me, and later I connected it to the fake news sites that pop up during elections. Many of these political bot farms were using similar tactics to try and drive attention (and clicks) to their disinformative "products."

The stories from Midori and Mercer reveal how users themselves, intended to be the passive targets of media platforms built by people like Lukas and defended by people like Danny, can actively respond to those platforms' attempts to manipulate their attention for profit; rather than simply being gamed, users themselves can game the media platforms in ways that were not predicted by their creators. The problem is not just that the employees at social media companies built their own biases into the tools they created or that they continue to enable the misuse of those tools because they refuse to recognize the problems. It's also that people looking for flaws in the system can use them for their own ends—including the end of spreading propaganda. In other words, these systems are not only as flawed as their developers but also as flawed as their users.

Social Media Is as Flawed as the People Who Create and Use It

As mentioned earlier, computational propaganda and manufactured consensus preexisted the exponential spread of social media.

The use of bots and other inorganic manipulation tools to amplify or suppress particular streams of political content was identified as early as 2010. According to Dev, these attempts to manufacture consensus have been going on since before today's social media existed; as I discussed in chapter 3, governments have been doing versions of this since there has been a mass media. But the world's major social media firms dismissed these problems right up until the 2016 U.S. election, which forced them to acknowledge it. Before that election, research teams around the globe—including the computational propaganda project I was working on—had already been trying to communicate the scope of the problem and its potentially devastating consequences to social media companies, both with rigorous empirical research and through semi-formal conversations. Before 2016, though, in the rare instances that I got a chance to talk to people from Facebook, Google, or Twitter at conferences or workshops, they either attacked my research or ignored it. Later, from 2017 onward, the same firms were scrambling to hire researchers and PhDs with knowledge of political manipulation and disinformation. But by then, the horse was out of the barn. It was too late for any group of technology companies, policymakers, or researchers to easily stem the tide of disinformation and digital political manipulation.

As the stories in this chapter make clear, people working at social media firms instill their products with their own norms, values, and beliefs. At the same time, people who use the tools discover ways to manipulate them into doing things not intended by the original builders. These two facts have serious implications when it comes to considering how and why computational propaganda is thriving in these new media ecosystems. Facebook, WeChat, YouTube, KakaoTalk, Twitter, Reddit, WhatsApp, Instagram, and other platforms like them are made to facilitate social networking, allowing people to build connections through various means of communication: text posts, videos, memes, and audio clips. In other words, people create their own content on these websites and software applications. And these companies rely on defining themselves not as content creators or content curators but as neutral platforms that simply host this user-created content. This is why section 230 of the U.S. Communications Decency Act specifies that internet companies in the United States are not responsible for the content that appears on their platforms. If hate speech, illegal pornography, or propaganda showed up in their chatrooms (the social media of choice back when 230 was penned), it wasn't Yahoo's, MSN's, or AOL's fault.

We now know this logic is deeply flawed. As the stories from my research reveal, software and internet platforms do regulate and shape content in some ways, particularly via the curation involved in recommendation algorithms. The social media companies' own employees know that their software infrastructure—trending, recommendation, and other related types of algorithms—encodes the biases of the people that built it. It is clear that social media websites and applications are not just passive vessels for hosting content created by their users. Just as NBC makes decisions about what programs to air during primetime, YouTube makes calls about what videos to recommend to users in their sidebars. And users too are learning to exploit the platforms' weaknesses. Social media systems are thus biased at both ends: they embody the flaws of both the people that build them and the people that use them. It is never simply accidental when certain kinds of political information spread on social media. As in Herman and Chomsky's day, several filters lead to powerful propaganda flowing over social media: size/consolidation, the advertising business model, and so on.

The sheer size of social media companies means that the firms are unable to effectively uncover all of the manipulation occurring on their sites. At the same time, their profit orientation disincentivizes them from rooting it out. They make money from ads, and the more eyes (even bot eyes) on ads, the more money the companies make. This is true for political advertising specifically; as with other forms of mass media, on social media, "the advertisers' choices influence [the media company's] prosperity and survival," and so certain kinds of political advertising content flies while other content dies.[18] Companies like Twitter have made moves to ban direct political advertising outright, and any social media employee will be quick to tell you that only a small portion of their revenue comes from direct political advertising from campaigns or governments. But now that we understand propaganda and manufactured consensus, it is clear that many of the folks working to manipulate public opinion over social media aren't part of those groups. As social media monopolies grow and command greater amounts of our attention, this will only become more true. When people spend more time on social media, they see more ads, and the companies make more money. Companies therefore seek to maximize the time users spend on the platform (also maximizing users' exposure to propaganda) rather than optimizing for, say, strengthening democracy or increasing user happiness.[19] To do otherwise is to lose money.

There are other financial incentives for social media companies to allow the websites and applications they maintain to spread propaganda—or at least to spread unchecked. Any media firm needs "a steady and reliable flow of the raw material of news," and social media companies are now in the business of recycling and hosting content from thousands of other media companies.[20] Many of these outlets are heavily biased, and their reporting may be pure overt propaganda. Even in the era of legacy broadcast media, when television reigned supreme, it was difficult for broadcast companies to make sure their shows didn't contain serious political bias; then, as now, some media companies' reporting was designed to serve the interests of their owners, shareholders, and advertisers. Today, social media companies have foolhardily taken on the challenge of moderating the content flowing out of those firms and from numerous other media.

Even those media outlets that are not intentionally spreading propaganda and disinformation are recycling "news" sourced on Facebook, YouTube, QQ, and other companies, which comes directly from their users. But as we have seen, the content that users share (whether original or from other sources) is always biased. In addition, the content that rises to the top is dictated by users' preferences: these media companies use insights about user behavior to prioritize all kinds of decisions, including not only trends and recommendations but also things like user experience—how the front end of a platform appears to those that use it. And the user interface itself shapes how users interact with and use the site. Recall the discussion in chapter 4 of how the differing fundamental structures of Facebook and Twitter produce different kinds of social connections. While the idea that news content should be spread based on users' choices would appear to be a kind of democratic decision-making, algorithms, site structures, and security loopholes mean that it is not. In fact, the notion of direct democracy—the idea that each person has an equal and direct say in each political decision—is itself flawed, and not just on the internet. The philosophers behind modern democracy understood that democracy cannot function without representation, a system of checks and balances, and robust law, and I would extend this insight to social media. It too requires these things to function well and to keep the inevitable bad actors from exploiting the system. In the early days of social media, building a new, "social" kind of media probably seemed simple: just bring together people online and let them share whatever content they like, then use mathematical systems to recommend content to those people. It turns out to be a lot more complicated than the companies bargained for. The companies that have put themselves in this position—and who are making billions of dollars in that position—are now complicit in and integral to the propaganda system.

This complicity is intensified by the issue of *flak*: social media companies' revenue streams depend on the goodwill of advertisers, and so they must constantly cater to the whims of advertisers, politicians, shareholders, and a wide variety of other interest groups, including regulators. Because they operate across national borders, the larger social media applications are beholden to a variety of masters. If Rafael Correa or his cronies push Twitter to overlook some of their political bot accounts, might not the company play ball? If Narendra Modi asks WhatsApp to not factcheck particular BJP WhatsApp groups, would they take the risk of losing money if they demur? If Walmart or Procter & Gamble—among the biggest advertisers on social media—asked YouTube to change up its ad practices, might YouTube not listen to the customer? Of course, social media firms always have the option to say no to flak—and they certainly have enough money to hold their own in lawsuits brought to threaten them into particular actions. But in the years I've spent doing fieldwork on computational propaganda, I've seen lots of evidence that the whims of the powerful (including those of the companies' own founders and C-level executives) are bowed to more often than not.

Social media's susceptibility to computational propaganda is thus baked into its design: the code that underpins platforms, the revenue model they depend on, and the fundamental vision that drove the sites' design. Social media is designed to provide anonymity and broad access online. However, we now know that these things tend to foster polarization among its users, increasing opposition between people and groups who disagree.[21] Social media refines one of the core tools in the manufacture of consensus: the use of the adversary or the other as a control mechanism. Social media firms prey on and intensify people's fears and xenophobia because they profit from engagement of any kind, positive or negative. This obviously drives the design of certain social media apps, like Gab or Parler, which market themselves as allowing unrestricted free speech (which, in practice, is usually explicitly racist, Islamophobic, and antisemitic speech—polarizing content "that even fairly laissez-faire sites like Twitter refuse to host").[22] But the larger social media firms also participate in this dynamic—another example of the social media/mainstream media ouroboros. In a study my colleagues and I did for the German Marshall Fund of the United States, we found that a great deal of the Islamophobic content we observed on Gab linked back to Facebook and YouTube.[23] The web is an interconnected network with no borders, and propagandists can effortlessly shift the same biased or hateful content from one site or app to another when they are kicked off one platform or when they want to extend their reach. And polarizing content—salacious, shocking content, including conspiracy theories—sells; social media companies have incentives to share shocking or infuriating content because clickbait content is engaging content—and therefore profitable content.[24,25]

When we look at all of these filters together—particularly company size and consolidation, dependence on ad revenue, and interconnection of the entire media system and its impact on sourcing—it is easy to see how, in combination, they leave space for bots, sockpuppets, and other forms of digital astroturfing. There is little incentive to track down automated social media accounts, which inflate the overall number of users of a platform and increase the platform's ad prices.[26] The companies' algorithms shape what information is sourced or highlighted on the platform. Bots and other forms of inorganic traffic can foster engagement by fostering divisions and polarization among users. As Yochai Benkler and colleagues and Philip N. Howard have pointed out, the flow of propaganda on social media is a cyclical affair, influenced by the intentions and interests of many groups: biased algorithms, loaded recommendations, and user decisions are all happening at once, and they all contribute to the problem.[27,28] This is part of why it is so difficult to fight back against disinformation and propaganda online. How can we battle what we can't pin down? How can we stop disinformation that comes from all sides—that is a feature, rather than a bug, of social media?

Companies like Facebook and Google are now among the most profitable firms in the world, and they are no less tied to powerful interests than any mass media company like Viacom CBS or Bertelsmann. A few years ago, I made a trip to Southeast Asia, where I met with several governmental stakeholders seeking advice about the problem of computational propaganda. Over dinner, one man, a leader of his country's foreign policy department, was extremely blunt about the power that states wield over social media companies. "What is a little country like ours to do?" he asked. "The Googles of the world now have much more power, and far more money, than we could ever hope for." We must face the fact that these companies—these giant corporations—are the linchpin of modern propaganda, and that susceptibility to propaganda is baked into their products and business models. But there are ways to mitigate the problem. As I discuss in the conclusion, a combination of regulation and accountability can help force social media companies to take their share of responsibility for the problem. By incentivizing practices and behavior that work against propaganda rather than foster it—by making it cost more to do nothing than to fix the problem—we can make progress toward a better digital media landscape and more democracy. We can also build new social media tools designed for democratic communication but less susceptible to control or manipulation by authoritarian regimes, trolls, and liars.

6

Journalism and Political Bots

As someone who specializes in field research and ethnography, I focus on spending time with the people I'm learning about. In the course of my career, I've spent countless hours doing what Clifford Geertz called "deep hanging out."[1] In Eastern Europe, East Asia, the Middle East, the Americas, Western Europe, North Africa, and Southeast Asia, I've talked to everyday users, small-time computational propagandists, hackers, academic experts, politicos, software engineers, and many more. But of all these crucial conversations with people deeply enmeshed in the computational propaganda ecosystem, one group of interviewees stands out to me: journalists. Reporters, more than any other group I've spoken to, have offered the most help in surfacing early clues about political bot use. They have also regularly and generously shared resources and tips about who to talk to and where to look for more interviewees.

Over the years, I've spent a great deal of informal time talking with newsmakers who are concerned with the growing propaganda problems associated with information and social media. (Perhaps this is one reason that I, a propaganda researcher, ended up in a School of Journalism; I often joke with my journalism school colleagues at the University of Texas that their job is to teach students what to do and mine is to teach students what *not* to do.) I've formally interviewed more than thirty journalists who either make and build their own bots—some as tools for their reporting, some for other purposes—or who specialize in the study of online propaganda and disinformation. I've spoken to numerous data journalists who specifically report on stories related to the elections. I have interviewed and hung out with investigative reporters and digital support staff who worked for major publications in numerous cities across the globe, including Brussels, Lagos, London, New York, Tokyo, and São Paulo. I spent time at news organizations learning about their efforts to build novel automated digital tools for journalists. I worked with newsmakers attempting to grapple with the effects of disinformation on the larger media environment. Over the course of my research, I've had literally thousands of conversations with journalists concerned with computational propaganda.

My time with these reporters has taught me three core things about the subject. The first is the most difficult to discuss, both because of my enormous respect for journalists and the work they do, and because I've come to understand the intense pressure they work under. But the fact is, journalists play a very real role in perpetuating manufactured consensus. It's not always—not even usually—done consciously, and much of it happens far above the level of the individual reporter. For example, many reporters are part of large media organizations (or massive media networks, like Sinclair) whose product continues to be molded by the various powerful actors and interests discussed by Edward Herman and Noam Chomsky.[2] This means that reporting perspectives are often guided by power.

For some reporters (perhaps especially those at smaller outlets, who do not have access to the resources of these massive mainstream media organizations), the problem is one of access and funding. Increasingly, reporters use social media as a reporting resource, not only because it's the preferred communication channel of many people around the world but also because they are under pressure to put out stories, and social media is an easy and accessible source of leads and information.[3] But given the reach of computational propaganda, sourcing news from social media can be a real problem. As discussed in previous chapters, the trends and numbers there can easily be gamed; perhaps worse, a great deal of information on sites like Twitter, Facebook, and YouTube is of dubious provenance, and reporters themselves can fall victim to manufactured consensus. Even digitally savvy reporters can be tricked by propagandists, and many of the computational propagandists I've spoken to spread disinformation with the *explicit goal* of getting journalists at major news outlets to report on the misleading content—and have succeeded.

For these propaganda makers and trolls, "mainstream" reporting on the latest incendiary Pepe the Frog meme or a jingoist, distorted, political tweet from a top politician is precisely what they want. It gives them wider reach and legitimizes their views. And it is working; in 2016, for instance, Robert M. Faris and colleagues found that the agenda of reporting around the 2016 election was effectively determined by the ecosystem of far-right media, including bloggers and social media personalities.[4] As Whitney Phillips puts it, "The takeaway for establishment journalists is stark, and starkly distressing: just by showing up for work and doing their jobs as assigned, journalists covering the far-right fringe—which subsumed everything from professional conspiracy theorists to pro-Trump social media shitposters to actual Nazis—played directly into these groups' public relations interests."[5] And this is happening across the globe. Interviewees described similar efforts to shape media agendas and narratives from the cyber militias in Brazil and BJP IT cells in India to the web brigades in Russia and Ukraine and the troll armies in Mexico.

The second thing I've learned while working alongside journalists is that they are among the primary targets for harassment campaigns from both state-sponsored trolls and automated political influencers. The overwhelming majority of journalists I've come to know through my research are doing the jobs they do because they believe in the work. They do it because they see real value in getting information to the public, in holding public figures accountable, and in uncovering the truth. They certainly don't do it for the money or for accolades and appreciation from society. Reporters who work for bosses like Jeff Bezos, who now owns the *Washington Post,* or Rupert Murdoch, who owns Fox News and the *Wall Street Journal,* know that they are constrained by their leaders' economic and political interests. But they do their jobs to the best of their abilities anyway. This is why they draw the ire of the worst sort of computational propagandists. People with allegiances to a wide variety of political groups (including official governments, both democratic and authoritarian) have reasons to want to silence journalists. Computational propaganda has become one of the core weapons in their arsenal for doing so.

The third and final thing I've come to understand through my fieldwork is that journalists are on the front lines of the fight against computational propaganda. Indeed, in this fight, they have adopted some of the weapons of the propagandists themselves; they often use automated and code-driven tools such as social media bots for their work, where they function either as social scaffolding (connecting people) or as a civic prosthesis (disseminating data and findings) for their reporting.[6] Yet here too code reflects the biases of their creators. The messages sent via journalism bots are subjective, and these automated reporting tools undoubtedly reflect the values of the reporters that help to build them, just as the algorithms behind Facebook reflect the values of its engineers. Are journalism bots a version of computational propaganda? By my definition, most are not; bots are only spreading computational propaganda if they lack transparency about their nature and builders, and if they communicate biased and deceptive information. Generally, the journalism bots I've seen used by reporters are encoded with ideals of transparency and honesty rather than opacity and partisanship. While all of us have biases, journalists have been working for years to mitigate theirs; they seek to report objectively, and if they cannot, their reporting is transparent about their positionality and politics.

The journalists I've encountered in my work are oriented toward helping to address the problem of manufactured consensus, not toward perpetuating it. But they still have work to do when it comes to not spreading computational propaganda. In the following section of this chapter, I discuss what not to do in the era of anonymity and automation—thoughts that should help journalists avoid accidentally spreading computational propaganda or helping to manufacture consensus.

How Journalists Perpetuate Manufactured Consensus

In September 2020, NBC News released a report titled "Russian Internet Trolls Hired U.S. Journalists to Push Their News Website, Facebook Says." It transpired that government-affiliated trolls, working for the now well-known Internet Research Agency (IRA), had hired a range of foreign and domestic journalists to report for a propaganda website named Peace Data.[7] The FBI alerted Facebook to the IRA website, and the social media company quickly worked to reduce the site's presence on their applications and sites. The IRA site, which was still working to grow its reader base when caught out, looked like a regular news site, but its features—reports on environmental concerns and political corruption—were aimed at dividing left-wing U.S. voters. According to Nathaniel Gleicher, Facebook's head of cybersecurity policy, the website was designed to evade common detection techniques. "You can run a loud, noisy influence campaign like the one we saw in 2016, and you get caught very quickly. Or you can try to run a much more subtle campaign, which is what this looks like," he said.[8]

The freelance U.S. journalists who had written for the site said they did so because they paid reasonably well—two hundred dollars per article—and that they hadn't known the site was run by the IRA. "I lost my job during COVID and was pretty desperate to earn money just to pay rent," one commented.[9] However, not all of the journalists writing for Peace Data were real. Some, including editors, were discovered to be false personas. According to cybersecurity researcher Lee Foster, who works for the firm Mandiant, the fake profiles used pictures created using deep fake technology—AI tools that mash together various facial features of different people to create a unique, highly realistic headshot. The use of real journalists alongside the fake ones lent legitimacy to the site; just as cyborg bots—hybrid automated/human accounts—are much more difficult to identify than fully automated bots, the Peace Data site was, as Foster noted, more difficult to identify as an influence operation because some of the content was from real journalists, with searchable bylines and legitimate publication histories.

This story shows how computational propaganda can be enabled or spread by genuine journalists. Although the website never had a chance to really take off, it was a top-down, Russian-led effort to leverage the reputations of real U.S. reporters to polarize the U.S. electorate. The real journalists who wrote for the site needed the money—something that is true for many freelancers in a time when reporters are being laid off or struggling to find full-time staff positions. The content they were asked to write also seemed fairly benign, or at least no different from other reporting they'd done elsewhere. But the IRA had particular political intentions and was targeting particular groups with the information it chose to publish.

There are many other stories of journalists' facilitating computational propaganda and manufactured consensus (though few are as clearly organized by a government group with particular political intentions). Reporters working for legitimate, highly respected news outlets have often spread bot- and sockpuppet-driven propaganda to the masses, whether intentionally or not. According to Josephine Lukito and colleagues, who analyzed "314 news stories that quoted at least one tweet posted by an IRA-controlled account," the "tweets were often embedded as vox populi, sharing opinions as if they were [from] regular U.S. citizens." They characterized this as "a loophole that allowed state-sponsored disinformation content to pass news gates."[10]

I've regularly encountered similar examples in my own work. In many circumstances, my interviewees told me they believed that governmental entities or government-paid organizations were using established news organizations to launder inorganic political information on social media. Other interviewees explained that extremist groups or even lone trolls were often successful in getting journalists to report on their propaganda. I saw some of these attempts myself. In 2018, I served as a Belfer Fellow for the Anti-Defamation League's Center for Technology and Society. During that time, I encountered many instances of antisemitic and white supremacist groups using bots, sockpuppets, and influencers' accounts to amplify their views, frequently employing subtle bigotry and dog whistles, over sites like Facebook, Twitter, YouTube, and Reddit. During the course of interviews for a report on digital antisemitism during the 2018 midterms, I realized that these groups were trying to get mainstream media to legitimize their content.[11] Many interviews with both propagandists and disinformation experts have borne this out, with interviewees telling me of seeing these same media targeting tactics in Brazil, Ecuador, France, India, Mexico, Ukraine, Taiwan, Spain, and Turkey.

There are many means of achieving what Joan Donovan and others have called "media manipulation."[12] First, as with the example of the Peace Data website, freelance journalists can be employed by organizations with unclear origins and intentions. It's difficult for reporters trying to make a living to turn down paid work, but examples like this make it clear that they should be on their guard. However, in my studies, I've rarely encountered this sort of direct payment system; it's much more common for propagandists to simply get journalists to amplify existing propaganda or disinformation than to fake a media organization and hire them. Reports that feature seemingly organic, "from the people" tweets that are allegedly from people on the ground during a political event are dangerous; this effort to show what "real" people think allows computational propaganda to be spread far beyond its original reach. This kind of sloppy reporting can have real consequences. A reporter should always contact a source and verify their identity before featuring their content in a story. Political bots and sockpuppet accounts are often purpose-built to manufacture consensus—to give the illusion that certain ideas have grassroots, organic popularity on social media. Reporters should not fall prey to this.

I've also seen journalists taken in by less direct methods of manufacturing consensus. For example, they report on trends generated by algorithms that have likely been gamed using bots and other forms of bogus traffic. After the Parkland shooting in Florida, the number one trending video on YouTube alleged that David Hogg was a "crisis actor" rather than a real student who had witnessed a real school shooting in which some of his peers were murdered. YouTube blamed their algorithmic system for spreading the video farther and faster than it should have gone.[13] Many media outlets—mostly false news sites, conspiracy blogs, or far-right outlets—used the video's apparent popularity to bolster their reporting that cast doubt on Hogg's background. Others journalists who wrote about the conspiracy to criticize it—either to decry YouTube's failure to catch and delete the trending video or to shame others for spreading the rumor—in fact boosted the video's reach by writing about it. The end result was the same, regardless of the intentions of the reporters who wrote about the video. In the words of Whitney Phillips, they lent the "oxygen of amplification" to a conspiracy theory driven, in part, by computational propaganda; automated amplification on social media begat amplification in the legitimate news media.[14]

This practice continues to be a problem, particularly in reporting on extremism and disinformation. In 2018, Joan Donovan and danah boyd revived calls for the "quarantining of extremist ideas."[15] They described the need for "strategic silence" among news outlets when it came to covering hate groups. "Newsrooms must understand that even with the best of intentions, they can find themselves being used by extremists," they wrote. They also noted that media could use their power to shape public discourse for good: "They have the power to defy the goals of hate groups by optimizing for core American values of equality, respect and civil discourse."[16] The same holds true for computational propaganda. News organizations and journalists must carefully consider the provenance of the information they report, the goals of the people asking them to report it, and the potential social impacts of their reporting.

How Journalists Are Victims
of Computational Propaganda

Journalists, as a group and as individuals, are among the primary targets of computational propaganda, which is used against them in three ways. First, propagandists seek to harass journalists into silence, leveraging cascades of violent threats and slander against them. Second, it seeks to drown out the voices of fact and reason that journalists represent. The group Reporters Sans Frontières is blunt about what the introduction of noise into the system does to democratic communication: "The virtual applause from bots and fake posts threatens the integrity of the public debate by drowning journalistic content and creating a content asymmetry."[17] Third, computational propagandists work to convince journalists to unwittingly share false content and thus help to manufacture consent. As I have shown, journalists' stamp of approval unlocks the door for computational propagandists: "Against a backdrop of polarization, the false information spread by bots is then read and shared by real activists"—the key mechanism for the manufacture of consensus.[18]

Bot-driven harassment seeks to intimidate reporters into silence. Ilana, a reporter for a European publication, was the target of one of these campaigns. One morning, she woke up to thousands of notifications on Twitter. A swarm of clearly automated accounts were targeting her with repetitive harassing messaging—and though they were repetitive enough to betray that they were bot messages, they were still upsetting and harmful. Perhaps the worst part for her was the seemingly regular users who answered the bots' call and began to dogpile her as well. It continued for weeks.

In chapter 3, I described several instances in which journalists from a wide variety of countries and backgrounds were targeted for harassment by automated propaganda, including political botnets, inorganically spread social media disinformation campaigns, and state-sponsored trolling efforts. These are but a small handful of the hundreds of similar cases I've heard about over the years. I have been given detailed accounts of computational propaganda attacks against journalists over nearly every major social media platform—from Twitter to Weibo, from KakaoTalk to Pinterest. Efforts to target journalists over social media using the tools of computational propaganda are spreading to new digital domains, shifting from major web 2.0 platforms such as Facebook and YouTube to encrypted communication applications such as Signal, Telegram, Viber, WhatsApp, and Zoom.[19]

Many computational propaganda attacks come from extremist groups or automated political influencers. While these are often fueled by false statements from state leaders using social media, some computational attacks on journalists actually originate from governments, and these are especially concerning. Given their resources, they can launch and legitimize the targeting of journalists at a huge scale. Government-sponsored attacks on journalists make up part of what seems to be a deliberate top-down campaign to erode public trust in journalism. In addition to personal attacks on journalists enabled by computational propaganda, bots push false news, disinformation, and misinformation to undermine the flow of quality information and therefore the public trust in journalism as an institution. This was the focus of a powerful joint statement from several international bodies, including the UN Special Rapporteur for Freedom of Opinion and Expression, the Organization for Security and Co-operation in Europe's Representative on Freedom of the Media, the Organization of American States's Special Rapporteur on Freedom of Expression, and the African Commission on Human and Peoples' Rights Special Rapporteur on Freedom of Expression and Access to Information. They said, in part, "[We are] alarmed at instances in which public authorities denigrate, intimidate and threaten the media, including by stating that the media is 'the opposition' or is 'lying' and has a hidden political agenda, which increases the risk of threats and violence against journalists, undermines public trust and confidence in journalism as a public watchdog, and may mislead the public by blurring the lines between disinformation and media products containing independently verifiable facts."[20]

As Nicholas Monaco and colleagues show, leaders from Bahrain to the United States have harnessed the power of social bots to defame the press, saying that "fake news is often only one element of a broader politically-motivated attack on the credibility and courage of dissenting voices: journalists, opposition politicians and activists."[21] As these international expressions of concern show, political actors around the world have consistently leveraged social media bots and other tools of computational propaganda to harass and silence individual reporters and the fourth estate more broadly. These attempts to undermine public trust in journalism have been very successful, as the constant refrain of "fake news" in the United States shows.

Here are a few examples (chosen from a nearly innumerable list) of bot-driven offensives on journalists, news organizations, and particular strands of reporting: in 2014, hordes of pro-Putin bots tied to Kremlin subordinates worked to confuse and overwhelm the *Guardian* and its readers in the comments sections of articles about Crimea.[22] In 2016, just a month before the U.S. presidential election, political bots and networks of sockpuppet accounts run by right-wing political groups were used to harass and threaten Jewish American journalists over Twitter.[23] In 2017, employees at the investigative news site ProPublica were tormented with bot-driven Twitter posts and "e-mail bombs" (which overwhelmed the outlets' e-mail systems—a form of direct denial of service) in response to reporting on technology companies, including PayPal and Amazon, whose products were enabling extremist groups to operate online.[24] In 2018, Saudi government bots drove a smear campaign against murdered journalist Jamal Khashoggi and helped promote an Arabic hashtag that translated to "we all have trust in Mohammed Bin Salman," which became a top global trend on Twitter.[25] Also in 2018, YouTube bots worked to downrank news stories criticizing Russia ahead of Putin's fourth "bid" for reelection.[26] In June 2020, the director of the

Mexican federal news agency Notimex was caught deploying "sophisticated bots" on Twitter to attack a number of journalists, including Carmen Aristegui, a well-respected Mexican reporter; the attack got the hashtag "#ApagaAristegui" ("turn off Aristegui") trending.[27,28]

In these instances, automated social media accounts drowned out journalists' voices, confused the public about the particulars of given stories, drummed up antijournalism sentiment, and promoted political groups and politicians. And these bots were just the tip of the propaganda iceberg—one tool among many used in attempts to manufacture consensus against the fourth estate. Sockpuppet accounts and organized groups of people leveraging their personal social media accounts were often used to amplify the bot-driven offensives against journalists, and regular people were also brought on board via the manipulation of trending and recommendation algorithms. This onslaught further manipulated the trends and recommendations, making it more likely that the whole thing would be reported in the mainstream media. The whole cycle becomes a campaign waged by the broader media ecosystem. This is exactly the kind of perfect storm of interconnected propaganda that occurred during the 2016 U.S. election.[29]

As I mentioned in the introduction (and as many other scholars have pointed out), it is nearly impossible to measure how well these tactics are working on everyday users of social media.[30] However, there have been some clear, measurable, real-world effects from these campaigns. For example, political bots helped make the manufactured scandal "Pizzagate" go viral in 2016.[31] This conspiracy theory, spread through social media from Reddit to Twitter, suggested that Hillary Clinton and other major Democratic figures were engaged in an illicit pedophile sex ring housed in a pizza parlor in Washington, DC. Tomas, a freelance journalist based in Europe, told me that when he began to dig into the Pizzagate story, he found that many of the accounts central to spreading it on Twitter appeared to be automated: they messaged hundreds of times a day about the same content, lacked basic profile information, and were followed by large numbers of similar accounts. Jonathan Albright, a professor at Columbia, described the role of social media automation in Pizzagate: "What bots are doing is really getting this thing trending on Twitter, [they] are providing the online crowds that are providing legitimacy."[32] They were, in other words, manufacturing consensus. The Pizzagate "scandal," propelled by automation and human sharing over multiple social media platforms, was picked up and covered widely in the U.S. and international media, and eventually a Pizzagate believer showed up at the pizzeria waving around a gun in an attempt to "save the children."[33,34]

Another 2016 case, in which bots were used to attack Jewish journalists, also had clear real-world effects, though not as stunning as a conspiracy nut waving a gun around a pizzeria. Instead, the attacks plainly slowed, and in some cases stopped, these journalists' reporting on the movement they believed were behind the attacks: the alt-right, a digitally savvy group that is publicly represented by well-dressed young men—a repackaging of white supremacy in ways that appeal to other young men online. June, a researcher who studies information operations, told me she had spoken to several of the journalists who were attacked. She felt that the "#thelist" attack was especially effective because most of those targeted chose not to report that they had been attacked, and many stopped reporting about the alt-right entirely. In other words, the attack served to "chill" the reporting on the investigation's targets. Legally, a "chilling effect" is the result of an action that "inhibits the exercise of first amendment rights."[35] The goal is to force journalists offline, either through fear or frustration— in other words, to stop their speech, to censor them. Many of my colleagues—academic researchers and others—have been similarly relentlessly attacked over social media by combinations of bots, sock-puppets, and real people. I myself have been a victim of this kind of harassment, receiving threats over Twitter and via e-mail. In 2017, I received a number of e-mails from accounts self-identified as Russian saying things like "we are watching you." This made me reluctant to report on Russian propaganda efforts for a time.

The tactics used to attack journalists in one country spread across national borders, for there are no borders online. According to propagandists I've talked to in India and Mexico, it is common for those initiating bot offensives to learn new methods for attacking journalists from global peers; propagandists and political bot builders often collaborate with one another, and techniques used in one context can be picked up and weaponized against a reporter living thousands of miles away. For instance, the tactics used in the hybrid bot-human journalist attack campaigns I've studied in Turkey seem to be informed by earlier efforts in Syria. Indeed, attack campaign techniques are apparently borrowed and adapted just like bot-making techniques, according to my conversations with bot makers and bot trackers targeting journalists from multiple countries (Mexico, Ecuador, Ukraine, and the United States).

How Journalists Fight Back Against Manufactured Consensus

Two thousand sixteen was the year of the bot. As much of the above discussion has shown, it was in the end of 2016 that the U.S. elections first brought bots into the public eye, as they played the villain of the larger story about interference in an election. For technologists, though, 2016 started off rosy. They were bullish on bots. Executives from the world's biggest tech firms, including Microsoft CEO Satya Nadella, were excited about chat bots (and social media bots), which they positioned as the technological successor to the wild success of the "app" (applications meant to be run on mobile phones, often as alternatives to more resource-intensive browser versions with similar functionality).[36] At Microsoft's World Partner Conference 2016, Nadella said that "the evolution of user behavior [in] computing will naturally involve the use of chatbots as the underlying basis for communication between user and information."[37]

For Microsoft and companies like it, investing in a wide variety of social bots made a lot of sense: they could be used as social scaffolding or infrastructure that allowed conversation and connections across a particular platform (or between platforms), on either the front or the back end. They could serve as automated conduits for user communication. For instance, they could be used to carry out some of the work that human customer service agents were paid to do. More than that, companies envisioned bots' supplanting apps by offering an all-inclusive, AI-enabled personal assistant experience (Siri, Alexa, Cortana, Google Assistant) rather than a static platform where users had to do all the searching and analysis themselves. Nadella and his peers situated bots as the key way to keep users within the Microsoft (or Amazon, Apple, Facebook, etc.) ecosystem, rather than having them bounce from app to app, from app to search engine, or from website to website.

Looking back, this fervor seems somewhat overblown. It has certainly died down since, for a variety of reasons. The reason most central to this book's subject is the growing distrust of bots as a group. In the aftermath of the 2016 election, much of the public now sees bots as digital "boogeymen," tools behind some of the largest disinformation and political manipulation campaigns to date.[38] This has created something of a PR nightmare for the term *bot*. Indeed, Silicon Valley has now mostly shifted its terminology, rebranding bots as "AI-" and "machine learning–"enabled communication systems.

Yet, as I've said, bots are not problematic in themselves, though they can be put to problematic uses. Indeed, some journalists are seeking to fight fire with fire—to use bots to fight *against* disinformation bots. Tech companies and journalists are thus quietly iterating on methods for using bots to respond to computational and networked propaganda.

How did the excitement around social bots as "social scaffolding" begin? Many large companies and startups originally built their businesses with the intention of leveraging social bots as crucial infrastructure. The chat platform Slack, launched in 2013, allocated $80 million to a fund geared mostly toward supporting bot-driven startups; millions of that were invested by the platform in eleven bot-making companies in the first six months of 2016 alone.[39] Also in 2016, Facebook began working to make chatbots core infrastructural elements of their Messenger app, and Amazon and IBM quickly followed suit.[40,41] Simultaneously, the digital news organization Quartz launched its Bot Studio (now AI Studio), and the Associated Press (AP) began using bots to actively write stories.[42,43]

During the same period, certain journalists, especially those reporting on tech and using computational analyses alongside their reporting, also began using bots for their personal and professional communicative needs. For journalists, as for big tech, social bots were a way to streamline their communication with users on the front end, and their back-end bot equivalents allowed them to parse large datasets. Again, journalists rarely refer to them as bots anymore, since the notion of bots is now tainted by their association with propaganda in the public consciousness. Instead, journalists often refer to AI-enhanced reporting. But the means and ends are the same: bots of all types continue to be used as reporting aids. The journalist bot builders I've spoken to build automated scrapers that search for leads on political corruption across the web, they construct search-bots to interrogate massive troves of financial information, and they use front-end social media bots to share what their other automated creations have found.

In many ways, journalists were ahead of tech companies in figuring out the communicative usefulness of bots. Numerous journalist bot builders have been tinkering with social bots on Twitter and Facebook since the early days of those platforms. According to Diana, a researcher and designer working at a major newspaper, bots have been crucial journalistic tools since the early days of the public web, when they helped reporters understand the profusion of online data (which was already an avalanche, even before the era of "big" data).[44] By 2016, journalists at her organization and others like it were using bots to automatically "communicate with people around the U.S. about the election." One of these election bot creations had two functions. People could ask the bot questions about the election—what the latest polls were, for instance—and it would retrieve the answer for them. They could also use the bot to communicate with the newsroom, asking journalists questions about their stories or giving them leads. Flagship papers in the United States such as the *New York Times* and *Washington Post*, as well as newer web-based publications such as BuzzFeed, were experimenting with using bots to gather and report information about the presidential race.[45] "Journalism bots" were active across Facebook, YouTube, Weibo, and Twitter, as well as emergent social media and closed-network chat apps like Slack, Facebook Messenger, Telegram, and WhatsApp. Quartz launched their bot studio in November 2016, just weeks after the election.

Despite the "bot backlash" in public sentiment after the U.S. election, journalists are still using bots. In 2018, the Australian Broadcasting Company partnered with the Hearken audience engagement platform to produce a Facebook Messenger bot that asked South Australians what they wanted to know prior to election day.[46]

Around the same time, "a text-generating 'bot' nicknamed Tobi produced nearly 40,000 news stories about the results of the November 2018 elections in Switzerland for the media giant Tamedia—in just five minutes."[47] The Tobi bot created bespoke news articles in both French and German for all of the country's 2,222 districts. That same year, the Brazilian news site Jota, which specializes in covering the country's political institutions, built a Twitter bot named @ruibarbot to tweet out the anniversaries of important lawsuits. In the fall of 2020, the firm Automated Insights released a public, free version of its "news-writing bot" Wordsmith, which the AP has used to automatically produce stories.

So, numerous global news entities now leverage a wide variety of bots in their reporting as they seek to push back against the problems of computational propaganda. Bots allow them to scale their efforts in getting the news to the public, nudging the signal-to-noise ratio in the right direction. Some journalistic entities like the Poynter Institute have built bots directly aimed at addressing disinformation and propaganda, such as fact-checking bots that communicate with social media users who share bogus content in their feeds.[48] In my research, I've personally come across several examples of social bots doing this work—counteracting disinformation with factual information. Early in my time studying the makers and trackers of bots, I spoke to Andrew, a reporter working at a Qatari publication. Andrew had built several Twitter bots to share objective facts in response to misleading comments from politicians. He called these journalism bots "information radiators"—a useful term that describes many of the use cases of journalistic social bots. The information radiator is best defined as an automated online string of computer code deployed by a journalist to more effectively—even continuously— report on stories using social media and other internet-based communication tools. What, Andrew mused, should a journalist do with all the information that came across their desk, much of which they would not have time to fully report on in-depth? How could the journalist get the masses of information relevant to the public, such as politicians' voting records, out to citizens without writing stories? And how could they reach more citizens with this information than they would be able to with traditional stories? This is where Andrew saw bots fitting in: they could be used to facilitate updates, share data, or report on simple stories.

This use of the bot as an information radiator highlights the difference between propagandists' and journalists' bot use: the intention. Are they being used to support transparency and democratic values, or are they being used to promote (the illusion of) consensus? Journalists talked about their bots as extending their ability to report facts or to make information more transparent—as supporting democratic values. Andrew, for example, reiterated over and over that his Twitter bots were holding democratically elected officials accountable for their actions by publicizing how they had voted on a bill or what they had said about a particularly controversial topic. This is diametrically opposed to how control-oriented political groups and individuals spoke about using bots; these groups discussed bots in terms of how they made their pet ideas seem popular or made them money.

In addition to their uses as information radiators, bots can support the journalistic endeavor in other ways. First, bots can act as social scaffolding to link readers to newsrooms and individual journalists—groups that might otherwise have difficulty connecting. As Diana put it, readers could interact with the bots that she and her team had built and launched over social media by "ask[ing] a question, or [telling] a fact, that would then be relayed to the media organization's reporting team to then be either answered or analyzed."[49]

Second, bots can help reporters streamline their work and make it more efficient. According to a journalist I interviewed named

Shelon, using social media bots to automate repetitive tasks freed up time for important tasks like writing, interviews, and investigation of stories. For Shelon, the most interesting function of the journalism bot was as a stand-in or proxy of the journalist.[50] She told me that bots could do the mundane work of automated online "heat-seeking": cataloguing the latest trends on different platforms, searching spreadsheets for important information, or updating social media feeds with new stories. Bots can help navigate the enormous amount of information online to be parsed, directing journalists to the most relevant content. For example, a bot might be built to fetch other writing related to a topic. Diana told me that "in an age where data leaks and whistleblowers are as technologically oriented as they are revealing, bots can crawl through thousands of pages online—searching for names, phrases, words, or numbers."

Perhaps the most innovative (and controversial) use of journalism bots is in the area of producing actual newswriting. Some people have argued that bots can quickly produce valuable news during political events and will likely play a key role in the future of political reporting.[51] Others are more conservative. According to Tetyana Lokot and Nicholas Diakopoulos, who have proposed a typology of "news bots," the usefulness of bots in the areas of automated commentary and opinion writing is limited, though they note that these automated tools could prove useful for niche journalism or local reporting.[52]

Lokot and Diakopoulos see news bots as potentially transformative for the modern media environment. However, they focus primarily on bots' function—the pragmatics of their use cases—rather than on broader questions of aims, effects, and ethics. Those journalists who seek to use bots to foster (rather than hinder) democracy must constantly engage in vigorous self-critique, for we must always remember that *people* construct these digital tools, encoding their own cultural values. Pan, an educator who builds bots, was particularly reflexive about the journalism and commentary bots that he and his colleagues constructed. Unlike the bots built by many journalists I spoke to, which were designed to produce objective updates about current events, Pan's bots were built to make political commentary. One of his creations, for instance, accessed facts from both past and present to critique Trump's policies. Pan told me that he thought a Twitter bot was a good, "fairly easy, automated, and functional" way of posting criticism. Pan sees himself not as a news reporter but as "a humanities research hound" who combines "intention, politics, and knowledge with research and the desire to do good."

Pan's creations are clearly opinion-oriented journalism bots, of the type that Lokot and Diapoulous said had limited utility. But it seems to me that Pan's bots do have utility; the problem may be one of definition, not of possibility. The opinion articles produced by bots might not look like those in the *Asahi Shimbun, El Pais,* or the *Wall Street Journal,* but they fit the definition of opinion writing: they use current events, news, and opinion to generate a form of critical reporting.

Synthesizing facts into critique and opinion is a complex task. Are bots up to this kind of complexity? Is this their best use, or should they automate repetitive tasks to free up human time for these higher functions? In other words, what best leverages bots' unique strengths and reduces the impact of their weaknesses? According to one bot designer I spoke with, bots work best when they are simple and single-function. On one of my trips to New York City during the 2016 U.S. presidential election, I was able to interview Leah, a journalist and designer, at the major U.S. news publication where she worked. Leah and her team had been building experimental interactive journalism bots for use during the 2016 election. The bots were designed to enable better one-to-one interactions between readers and reporters.

Leah, who had been working with bots for many years, said that she was interested in them for their "botness" as much as for their ability to "mimic people."

Leah wanted to use bots to push the boundaries of journalistic practice. She made it clear that bots were extremely useful tools for journalists searching or reporting on information. More interesting to her, however, was that their social functions and automation—alongside their relative freedom in interacting with ecosystems online—oftentimes pushed the boundaries of journalistic expectation. She said, "Bots are at their best and worst when they do things that we don't expect." Sometimes, bots surprised her; after being launched online, they revealed novel uses that she and her team had not even imagined. A bot designed to gather trending stories on a given topic and then share that information with both reporters and readers through social media, for example, sometimes surfaced bits of information reporters did not expect: discrepancies in polling data, newsworthy stories shared with the bot via a reader on Slack, or a penchant for unintentional news humor.

After experimenting with several types of news or journalism bots, Leah told me that she had come to the conclusion that bots should be both more nuanced and, at the same time, simpler. She felt that users should have input on how the bot interacted with them; they should not, for example, bug the user for input or become "spammy," like Microsoft's nearly universally loathed Clippy. If the user only wanted to see election poll updates, then the bot should be able to do just that, and the options for directing the bot's behavior should be limited and clear. As it was, she and her team had tried to do too much with the bots they had built—they had too many functions, many of which were confusing for readers and reporters alike. She believed that her bots would have been much more successful if they had discrete, personalizable uses.

Conclusion

What is the future of journalistic bots? And how can we separate "good" bots (such as journalism bots) from "bad" bots (such as propagandistic political bots)? One informant, a data journalist named Reke, was blunt in her assessment that this is a key task for the field of journalism bot usage. She was emphatic that more "tools are needed to work toward identifying and disarming" what she called "bad" bots and supporting "good" ones. One way to distinguish between the two types is to look at why a particular bot is being used. Journalists describe the purposes of their bots differently than computational propagandists (whether government-supported groups or individual automated political influencers) do.

The computational propagandists I spoke to focused on how bots could be used to amplify or suppress social media content on behalf of a particular candidate. What these groups produced were clearly, by the definition used in this project, political bots; they produced disinformation (which many now call fake news) and used armies of bots to boost their stories and manipulate public opinion. In contrast, journalists who used bots did so in order to present objective reporting, not subjective or manipulative content. Journalistic bots were sometimes used to automatically post new articles, but the bots were not netted together into armies, nor did the bot accounts pretend to be real people. More often than not, they were single accounts representing particular news organizations that were coded to update automatically, and most bots used by journalists at regional and national newspapers, magazines, and reputable online news publications identified themselves as bots.

Perhaps even more interestingly, the two groups of bot builders differed not only in the uses to which they put their bots but also in how they thought about bots as a category. Most of my journalist informants thought of bots purely in terms of utility—as tools.

When directly asked, some were willing to hypothesize about the subjective, personified elements of their creations, but when it came time to use bots for reporting, the journalists were not caught up in the ontological nature of bots—whether they were real or fake, human or robot. In contrast, campaign and candidate bot builders and digital constituent bot builders were quicker to personify their bots. They were much more likely to think of bots as fake automated profiles—as imitations of real people. These builders saw the utility of their creations, but they mostly used them to stand in an on-line gap where they needed apparent support of many users in order to give an idea or story the illusion of popularity. This difference is perhaps most neatly summed up by saying that generally speaking, computational propagandists think of bots as proxies for people—either for their creators or for the voices of imaginary people online, designed to create a chorus of agreement with a particular political cause or candidate. In contrast, journalists generally think of bots as information radiators—a role tied to the bot's utility, focused mostly on the bot's particular professional context.

Future work on the ways that journalists make use of bots should consider how bot reporting may itself be both implicitly and explicitly political. By focusing on the former idea—on how the act of using bots in reporting is a political act because reporting itself is never truly objective—scholars will more effectively delineate the differences between journalism bots and political bots. Examining the explicitly political nature of journalism bots will allow us to better distinguish between bots that are used to spread information and those that are used to spread disinformation. Work focused on the veracity of information on social media during future political events will be bound up with work on the role of social media bots in political communication.

Conclusion: Provocations, Solutions, and the Future of Manufacturing Consensus

Core Arguments and Concepts

Today, anyone can be a producer of propaganda, and anyone can be manipulated. Leaders—from Andrés Manuel López Obrador of Mexico to Vladimir Putin of Russia—leverage disinformation and slander, using tools ranging from legacy news outlets to encrypted messaging apps like Telegram, and boost their own agendas while undermining their opponents'. But propaganda has been democratized, and there is a growing array of tactics and technologies—from geo-propaganda to virtual reality—that can be used to target and sway those same global leaders in their turn. These tools are available to a grab bag of tech companies, extremist groups, and mercenary PR firms who seek to manipulate the other groups for their own ends—sometimes to make money off online ad markets or bankrupt their competitors, sometimes simply because they were hired to do so. The real game-changer, though, is that these same digital propaganda and targeting tools are available to the most ordinary people—the Little League coach down the street, the mail carrier on your block, the salesperson at Best Buy. All of these disparate groups, each with its own discrete set of motives, are working to manipulate people's opinions by manufacturing the illusion of consensus online.

Extending the propaganda model developed by Herman and Chomsky in the 1970s for the social media age, I have argued here that modern computational propagandists seek to manufacture consensus via the bandwagon effect.[1] This idea draws on theories of public opinion like Elisabeth Noelle-Neumann's spiral of silence, which says that people can be tricked or swayed but that they can also be wary of speaking out for other reasons.[2] While I have here accessed and adapted theories of propaganda from Lippmann, Bernays, Ellul, and other foundational scholars of the subject, I believe that more research needs to be done connecting contemporary propaganda efforts to communication theories such as Noelle-Neumann's.[3,4,5,6] Traditional models of propaganda do not take into account the co-ordinated harassment campaigns that are a key tactic in today's computational propaganda landscape. These harassment campaigns aim to drown out or silence those seeking to spread accurate information. The numerous journalists I've spoken to throughout the course of this work have been candid about the chilling effects of online ha-rassment and state-sponsored trolling campaigns. Indeed, the chill-ing effects of computational propaganda extend far beyond those people impacted by direct harassment campaigns. Many people, and especially many members of minority groups, have told me how the propaganda they encounter online makes them more skeptical of political conversation writ large, making them less likely to engage in civic participation—including voting—at all. In fact, this is pre-cisely the goal of a significant portion of today's computational pro-paganda, which seeks as much to introduce noise and chaos into the system and to divide citizens as it does to convince people to adopt a particular political stance.

In this book, I have laid out several working theoretical concepts I developed from my last several years of research among makers, trackers, and victims of computational propaganda. The first is the core idea behind this book: the manufacture of consensus. This is the notion that modern online propaganda campaigns aim to create the *illusion* of support for, or opposition to, a person. This illusion has real power in the world. Global leaders of democracies (perhaps especially those authoritarian-leaning leaders of democracies, such as Narendra Modi and Donald Trump) have benefited in immeasurable ways from the amplification of content that supports them and undermines their enemies, carried out by political bot, sockpuppet, and human armies. While computational propaganda has most often been used by (and benefited) right-wing governments, as with Modi and Trump, it has also been leveraged by authoritarians in communist or former communist regimes, as in China and Russia. It is rarer to see computational propaganda taking hold in stronger democracies like Germany or New Zealand, though political bots, sockpuppets, and other social media tools have been used by extremist groups and others in those countries too.[7] In the last ten years, these digital tools and techniques have both bolstered and torn down political systems from far-right populism to authoritarianism and progressivism.

Several questions are at the center of this book: Who is responsible for computational propaganda? Why do people spread it? And what does it do? The first question is a complicated one, and the answer is equally complex. We sometimes know who carries out certain campaigns. For instance, we know that governments around the world have used social media bots, sockpuppets, and partisan nanoinfluencers in strategic bids to control public opinion, and I've spoken to many regular people—automated political influencers—who use these same mechanisms to push their own views.[8] Are these campaign initiators the ones responsible for the spread of computational propaganda? Perhaps, but we also know that computational propaganda would be impossible without the platforms that help it thrive. The flow of propaganda and disinformation is shaped by social media firms, particularly their trending and curatorial algorithms. The employees at those firms, and especially their leaders, made intentional design choices that enabled propaganda, and they have been deeply negligent in trying to stop the problem—in part because they profit from it. Are they not also responsible for the spread of computational propaganda? But what about journalists? We know that they are a major element in the propaganda ouroboros—the cycle through which disinformation is laundered and legitimized by being brought into the mainstream news. Journalists too legitimize and perpetuate computational propaganda (though, as mentioned above, they also work to combat it). News outlets, like social media firms, are bound up in the attention economy. The more clicks a story gets, the more the *New York Times* benefits, and the shocking and infuriating (the itches that computational propaganda is designed to scratch) get views. Are journalists responsible for computational propaganda? I would say "yes": all of these sets of actors are partially responsible for the digital disinformation landscape in which we find ourselves.

The second key question is *why* people spread computational propaganda. As I've shown here, those who use bots and other tools to amplify or suppress certain ideas (including false ones) do so for two primary reasons: to spread political views or to make money—or both, for the two are not mutually exclusive. Generally, governments, politicians, political campaigns, militaries, and other state-based groups are motivated by the desire to spread political views; they use social media bots and sockpuppets to control the populace, either by spreading effusively pro-government messaging (as in China) or by attacking critical opposition (as in Turkey).[9,10] As a group, the individual bot makers and automated political influencers I spoke to were more difficult to pin down. While many were motivated primarily by money, some were motivated partially or solely by fervent political belief. The political Twitter bot builders I talked to in the United States and United Kingdom, for instance, were building their tools to boost support for a particular candidate (in 2016 and 2020, most often Donald Trump) or cause (for example, Brexit or Blue Lives Matter).

There is always a "why" to the deployment of computational propaganda that is necessarily intentional. However, as we have seen, it can be spread unintentionally, either by credulous regular users of social media or sometimes by journalists, who can spread or legitimize computational propaganda simply by reporting on it, even critically. After all, even negative attention is attention. But what about the role of social media companies? Can we say that their role in spreading propaganda is unintentional? If we give them the benefit of the doubt, we can assume they simply did not foresee their applications and websites being used for political manipulation. But these days, few people are inclined to give them the benefit of the doubt. As many of my interviewees have pointed out, social media firms benefit from having millions of bot and sockpuppet users on their platforms; the more users, the more overall ad engagement numbers and the stronger the bottom line. And these companies have now had years to deal with issues of disinformation and propaganda but have not addressed them in any meaningful way.

The third key question of this book is about effects. While we can't accurately measure the real effects of these campaigns on user behaviors, we can ask propagandists what impact they believe their campaigns have on elections and other political events. Some propagandists are more circumspect than others, unwilling to commit to saying that their campaigns produce any but the most benign and small-scale of behaviors—clicking on a link or liking a post. This is especially true of those bot builders who are in it for the money. Others report similar measurable outcomes (retweets and shares, especially by politicians and media levels) but crow about the reach and import of their work. The politically zealous bot and sockpuppet users, in particular, proudly report that their bogus automated and human accounts—or the messages they spread—have been retweeted or shared by politicians and media organizations at the highest levels.[11] According to this group, this kind of exposure helps their ideas become more widely accepted or recognized. In other words, these bot builders think that they are achieving their goals. They see their efforts as helping to manipulate public opinion and manufacture consensus.

Several secondary research questions also shaped the research in this book. How might bot technology be used for pro-democratic purposes—constructed and deployed to affect behaviors like voting and civic engagement? How are bots used by or against other democratic institutions, particularly the free press and nongovernmental organizations, to generate or influence content and communication? Evidence in this book gestures at answers to some of these questions, but more research is needed to fill out those answers. I am most concerned with how bots drive social change in ways that go against their builders' intentions or actions. How are bots challenging traditional notions of agency in science and technology studies and traditional concepts of actors in studies of political communication? One place to begin is with the exploration in chapter 4 of the bot's role as the proxy for its creator.

~~Arm~~Deskchair Punditry at Scale

Facebook and Twitter users are all too familiar with this character: the guy who is always arguing politics, no matter what the conversation is about. This behavior is endemic to the internet at large, which has democratized our access to information and to platforms that allow us to share that information. Regular citizens are now documentarians, podcast hosts, investigative reporters, and political pundits. Now, we are all Reply Guys.

In some ways, bots allow this type of deskchair punditry to scale; that guy can now reach enormous audiences with his opinions. But this is not a form of what Malcolm Gladwell has called "slacktivism."[12] These users are not using bots as a form of activism, to push people toward democratic ideals. Indeed, while the spread of online propaganda undoubtedly causes social change of some type, it is decidedly not the online *democratic* change touted by the original internet theorists. We know that false news and conspiracy theories travel quicker than truth on social media; it seems that the more democratic the access to the internet and its tools, the easier it is to spread lies.[13]

In fact, it is the most democratically structured sites (like Twitter), with open APIs and flexible automation policies, that most powerfully enable the spread of computational propaganda. During numerous elections and events around the world, ordinary people—not just powerful political actors—use bots to spread political content, which can range from fact-based journalism to outright disinformation. I spoke to one man, a citizen bot maker living in the Midwest, who maintained several servers and a fleet of computers in his own house. He was exactly the type of citizen propagandist I have introduced in this book, an automated digital influencer. Many people in India, Turkey, the United Kingdom, and elsewhere have told me similar stories (shared in chapter 4) about similar small-scale yet professional operations they've run.

But computational propaganda is not an entirely novel phenomenon. It is still propaganda, and it still fundamentally follows the model described by Herman and Chomsky. The biggest change since the late 1980s when they wrote their first book is that propaganda now happens at a previously unthinkable scale. This is primarily because of two new features of computational propaganda: anonymity and automation. Automation allows politically inclined groups or people to amplify their views—and to suppress the ideas of others.

Anonymity is perhaps even more revolutionary in its capacity to allow for the profusion and success of propaganda. It is nearly impossible, even for the social media companies (particularly if the platforms are end-to-end encrypted, like WhatsApp), to determine the provenance of information. This means that bot builders can not only scale their work using automation but do so without fear of being discovered. The same feature both protects democratic activists, masking their identities in oppressive regimes, and allows bad actors to manipulate public opinion.

Olaf, a bot builder who used both anonymity and automation to great effect in his efforts to spread his political ideas, claimed that he ran several thousand Twitter political accounts using automated software. He showed me several of these accounts; all had tweeted hundreds of thousands of times in their short lifespans, some more than a million. The scale of Olaf's operation was unique among the automated political influencers I spoke to. Most of the other influencers I interviewed ran ten, twenty, or at most a couple of hundred bot accounts on Twitter. Some simply used a few manually run sockpuppet accounts. But Olaf ran his operation like a political campaign (albeit smaller). He told me that his goal was to use Twitter to eventually become a pundit on traditional media. He thought that if he became famous for his political opinions on Twitter, then he could become famous on TV. There could be no clearer example of the multi-mediated manufacture of consensus.

Most people—including policymakers and technology leaders—see the problems posed by "fake news," bots, sockpuppets, and other facets of computational propaganda. But for the most part, there are no systematic solutions to the problem. Twitter and Facebook have cracked down on the usage of bots and the spread of disinformation, but neither these tech giants nor their users can prevent the spread of computational propaganda. And the propagandists are always a step ahead of the "white hats." The next big threat is perhaps the use of so-called deep fakes during elections and crises—AI-doctored images and video designed to manipulate public opinion. Some propagandists are already experimenting with spreading disinformation via virtual reality platforms.[14]

Computational Propaganda, Political Communication, and Science and Technology Studies

What is it about social media that makes it especially hospitable to propaganda, disinformation, and control? The answer may lie, at least in part, in Ronald J. Diebert's "three painful truths" about social media. First, he points out, social media is built to invade user privacy and to monetize that invasion; the social media business model is based on deep and relentless surveillance of consumers' personal data to target advertisements. Second, users are complicit in this transaction; we permit this staggering level of surveillance willingly, if not altogether wittingly. And finally, social media is far from incompatible with authoritarianism.[15] Contrary to the idealized vision of the internet as an inherently democratic tool, social media platforms are proving to be incredibly effective enablers of authoritarianism.[16]

As social media companies intensify their chase for profit (pivoting away from person-to-person communication to mass communication, privileging video and the sharing of links in its algorithms in an attempt to cannibalize the news industry), they seem to no longer even pretend to aspire to the internet's original promise of democratization. Recently, Twitter and Facebook have been normalizing top-down communications; political elites have figured out how to harness social media to exert power and control.[17] As campaigns have shifted online, and as digital tools have been picked up for campaign outreach, they've left people behind rather than bringing them along.[18,19] Politicians have also gotten savvy to the massive amounts of personal data people store online and have figured out how to use this information to tailor their propagandistic messages.[20] They harvest data on moldable publics from social media, through their own campaign apps, and using location-tracking tools like geofencing.[21]

In addition to using data to target particular groups of voters, organizations built in the mold of Cambridge Analytica are continuing to perfect means of weaponizing personal data to target individuals. Leaders like Modi and Trump use digital tools like Twitter and WhatsApp to put their messages directly into the ears of the people. As one informant, a social media expert named Cain, put it, "Trump used Twitter as a megaphone, as a tool to get his campaign message heard above all others." But Trump's (or his campaign's) success did not come from simply harnessing the communicative power of social media—using it the way it was designed to be used. His success comes in no small part from the democratization of propaganda and the microtargeting of campaign messages made possible by social media's collection of user data. These things have also been important to the success of Bolsonaro, Duterte, Erdoğan, and Modi. Together, politicians and campaigns (and their supporters) are creatively using social media, bots, sockpuppets, and other tools. When these mechanisms of computational propaganda exist alongside a slate of social problems, they set the broader agenda of the media and the public in their favor.

This book builds on previous arguments about evolving hybrid technology systems and a society in which communication, political and otherwise, is defined via the flow of information across an entire media ecosystem that entangles print, broadcast, and digital.[22] I extend this previous work, examining how automated tools, social media platforms, and online tactics ranging from disinformation to political harassment relate to traditional media and political institutions and traditional methods of political persuasion. As David Karpf points out, "even the most radical changes to communications systems must be channeled through [standing political] structural constraints to impact traditional political outcomes."[23] Some politicians and parties have figured out how to have the best of both these worlds—the radical change and the traditional political structure. Many old-guard members of the political elite remain entrenched worldwide and have adjusted to the altered state of political communication as it exists online. They have learned to use automated, anonymous digital tools to create more noise and confusion in online communication, drowning out accurate information and alternative viewpoints. Governments like Russia are using Cold War tactics, updated for the digital sphere: polarizing their adversaries, exploiting existing social divisions, "dividing and conquering" their enemies by splitting coalitions.

Of course, the opposition is fighting back using some of the same weapons. Journalists, media makers, and democratic activists also use bots and social media to increase the amount of signal in the noise: they spread factual investigative reporting, publicize instances of corruption or misconduct, and educate users in attempt to stem the tide of digital disinformation. Their accounts are transparently automated, used as "information radiators" on the front end; on the back end, they allow journalists to uncover crime and corruption by harnessing big-data analyses. People are realizing that we can't stop the automated flow of mis- and disinformation manually; we cannot fight the ever-stronger "firehose of falsehood" with the "squirt gun of truth."[24] We need firehoses of our own.

Yet perhaps we can also slow the firehose of falsehood by understanding the deep architecture of these social media platforms, and of the internet itself. This book follows previous scholars of communication and media in arguing that software algorithms are inherently political; these seemingly neutral bits of code affect our digital interactions in serious ways.[25] As Tarleton Gillespie points out, algorithms frame the information that people see and digest when they use social media.[26] Facebook, Twitter, and sites like them curate our news, deciding what we should read. They base these recommendations in part on the information or data they have gathered about us; in part on what benefits them financially (clickbait and material from advertising partners); and, in large measure, on layers and layers of previous subjective human decisions about what is important. In addition to these inherent flaws in recommendation algorithms, they can also be gamed; bots can trick trending algorithms on social media by pushing certain hashtags or videos, making it seem like a lot of real people are paying attention to something in order to manufacture the illusion of consensus.

The people I interviewed and spent time with to write this book were clear about this problem. They believed that algorithms and software code can work to enforce a particular politics—to discriminate based on social standing or ethnicity, to boost one side of the argument on gun control, women's reproductive rights, or global warming over another. Algorithms, software, and bots are now themselves a communications technology, like broadcast television or online newspapers, but they are also a social technology that is "caught up in the ways we ratify knowledge of civic life."[27]

Toward an Ethnography of Information

Algorithms, powerful as they can be, are simply a form of automation, and like algorithms, automation encodes some of the values of its creators. With this in mind, I believe we need to learn more about not only the *people* who build and use bots but also the bots themselves. One might call this an ethnography of human *and* semi-human actors. I say "semi-human" because while bots are not human, they are built by humans and reflect a little of that humanity as they serve as proxies for their creators. I think of my work as ethnography of techno-human culture—a hybrid culture driving social change that is informed by actors who are not always, or necessarily, human.

Spending time with nonhuman or semi-human actors is a challenge for ethnographers of information. In this research, I explored how an ethnographer might do deep hanging out in a community at least partially composed of political bots. I followed particular accounts over long periods of time, gathered data from these accounts, and took notes on how they engaged in political communication. I also spoke to the people who made and built these bots, and it is accounts of these interactions that make up the bulk of this book. In a sense, I engaged in traditional ethnography among humans engaged in communication alongside ethnography of information.

Of course, my notion of an "information ethnography" is still in its infancy, and I am not yet able to fully operationalize it as a practice. I believe that this new ethnography of information will be useful for scholars examining the communication practices of bots, of algorithms, of artificially intelligent robots, or of information technology systems more generally, but there are still many questions to be answered. How is ethnography of information both different from and similar to traditional ethnography? What can researchers learn from spending time with both makers of tools and the tools? Beyond this, how might we think about bots as something other than simply tools—especially when driving sociality in ways unintended by their creators?

The ethnographic study of political bots on sites like Twitter, Facebook, and YouTube is a challenge for several reasons. First, it is practically difficult to do. In this work, as I examined the difference between what political bots did online versus what builders intended these bots to do, I more often than not relied on data from human builders rather than from bot accounts themselves. This was in part because I found it overwhelming, and ultimately futile, to qualitatively track and interact with the tens of thousands of political bot accounts with unclear origins, which communicated in seemingly frantic non sequiturs and were constantly being deleted. Second, ethnography is built around the study of *human* culture—the norms, values, and beliefs of groups of people—and bots are not human. But they are often built to mimic—or at least proxy for—people, and they communicate with people. Despite the practical difficulties I encountered, bot accounts can be tracked, followed, and researched, their communication catalogued and analyzed qualitatively. But this work is generally much more useful, and bots' communicative intentions are much clearer, when the study of particular bot accounts is paired with fieldwork with the people who have built said accounts.

However, we can't always (or even usually) identify who built these bots, so we can't always use traditional human ethnographic methods to study them. An ethnography of information must ask: what is interesting about how bots and other information technology systems communicate and socialize *beyond* the intentions of their human builders? Here lies the purer analysis of the automated systems themselves, and their interactions with people who had no hand in their creation. It is fascinating that bots often respond unexpectedly to online interactions. But equally interesting is *bots being bots.* Bots' fully unhuman behaviors are able to drive sociality of both human and nonhuman communities. This book explores political bots (and political botnets), establishing them as specific units of analysis among scholars of communication in hopes of pointing to a road for future research: a fully realized ethnography of information. But until we can operationalize this idea of the pure ethnography of information, we can continue to study bots, their builders, and the societies and networks in which they are deployed using more traditional ethnographic methods.

Here, I have shown that politicized social bots are among the most important developments in the technologically oriented study of political communication. I suggest that academics, journalists, civil society groups, and the general public should continue to work to understand the ways these "coded" political automatons are affecting communication and society worldwide. Bots, in the simplest sense, are tools for communication, and political bots, which mimic real people on social media, can be considered a new form of media because they are used to transmit information from their builders to broader communities. Bots' communicative utility is only just beginning to be explored, and the discipline of communication must interrogate both bots writ large and political bots specifically, as emergent, important tools and as unique, semi-human actors.

Solutions: Technical and Social

How can we address the enormous social problem I have sketched in this book? One promising intervention might occur through policy and the law. In order to pass laws regulating firms where disinformation is spread, we need more empirical research into the effects of political bots. This can inform policy recommendations for key politicians, policy experts, civil society groups, and journalists. Solid research into the ways computational propaganda contravenes existing law is a crucial step in addressing the policy gap. How, for example, are campaign finance, election law, voting rights, privacy, and other areas of the existing law being affected by the spread of political disinformation over social media?[28]

Longitudinal work can help establish more solid metrics for tracking information flows related to the use of political bots, computational propaganda, and the corresponding disinformation and online polarization they foster. Quantitative insight into the roles of automation, network structure, temporal markers, and message semantics over social media can allow experienced researchers to create ways of effectively measuring the flow of political manipulation over social media across sustained periods. The results of this longitudinal research will be crucial to building evolving, long-term public and governmental understandings of computational propaganda.

Another possible intervention is technological. Obviously, *purely* technical solutions are not feasible (nor, from the point of view of the technology companies, desirable—remember how profit and liability constrain them). But some technical interventions can help. We need better software, informed by both social and computer science research, to help researchers, journalists, and activists keep up with the challenges posed by the modern disinformation threat. Tools could include high-powered data intelligence platforms that use bots to parse large sets of data; they should exploit recent advances in graph databases; machine learning; and cheap, massive computational power to dramatically accelerate investigations. These tools and the information they mine should be accessible to researchers, journalists, and activists worldwide. The aim should be to be able to rapidly identify (and stop) disinformation campaigns as they occur and to identify patterns of activity that would help to root out entities backing these disinformation campaigns.

The Future of Computational Propaganda

Where is computational propaganda headed? How are the people that make and launch bot, sockpuppet, and influencer-driven manipulation offensives evolving their techniques? What problems in this space are being addressed and which still need to be dealt with? How can we deal with the changing nature of attempts to manufacture consensus using well-known and emerging digital tools? Each question is well worth exploring in future research. I have attempted to answer some of these, particularly those around the evolution of computational propaganda and the tools used to perpetuate it, in *The Reality Game*.[29] Other questions, regarding policy and legal approaches in the United States, I've answered with former Federal Election Commission chair Ann M. Ravel and with my research collaborators.[30,31] Additional ones require much more exploration.

My current research team and I have noticed several worrisome trends in and around global propaganda. First, encrypted chat apps (like WhatsApp) and private chat forums (like Discord) are now being adopted globally at a much greater rate than more traditional open platforms like Facebook, Twitter, and YouTube.[32] These apps and forums are often used to communicate with friends and family—this is why WhatsApp group sizes are limited to 256 users. But this is precisely what makes them ripe for spreading political manipulation. These applications are now the preferred mechanisms for many propagandists, who use them for two reasons. First, the intimacy of connections—friends and family—on WhatsApp and similar tools makes them an ideal place to genuinely effect change (in the eyes of our informants, at least). This is because people are more likely to change their behavior in response to someone they trust and care about.[33] Second, the applications are secure, and therefore social media companies and government regulators cannot see "inside" the application to find and delete disinformation or to identify the people spreading it. The goal is to get people to misinform one another through WhatsApp, and then for the chat members to eventually spread that misinformation on open social media platforms. Facebook (which owns WhatsApp) has had some success at preventing this mis- and disinformation from spreading by placing new limits on people's ability to mass forward messages.[34]

Similar infrastructural changes will likely prove useful at combating this form of propaganda on private chat apps, and governments and third-party regulators and experts can work with social media firms to ascertain the success of such measures.

While the end-to-end encryption of these apps seems an easy target for regulation aimed at stopping disinformation, it would be a crucial error to outlaw such messaging applications. These private applications are useful communication tools for activists in both authoritarian and democratic regimes, allowing them to share information privately, and it is crucial that people have a means to organize in the face of repressive powers. But of course, the same encryption that protects democratic activists also allows terrorists to organize and propagandists and other malicious groups to secretly spread problematic content that can undermine democratic communication.[35]

Because of its positive uses, my colleagues and I do not suggest that policymakers should legislate the dismantling of end-to-end encryption; instead, they should look to specific ways that these particular digital media are being used by propagandists and seek to block or hinder only those efforts. These chat applications are—by design—siloed environments. The people we've spoken to who use them to spread malicious content do so hoping that users will eventually spread (and amplify) that information through larger, unencrypted social media sites, and from there to traditional media outlets. However, without the ability to spread their disinformation or manipulation to more broadly used media, propagandists are stymied. The key is to catch the propaganda in transit—as it spreads out of an app like Telegram but before it goes viral on a site like YouTube. For other uses of end-to-end encryption communication channels, such as for terror or organized crime, law enforcement agencies must look to other arenas to discover illicit coordination. They can leverage the fairly robust amount of metadata collected by these and other private chat platforms. They must not, however, continue calls to dismantle encryption. There is a line where our right to private communication must be drawn, and this is it. You cannot give a so-called back door into end-to-end environments without irreconcilably compromising the system.

Another arena of concern for my research team lies in the use of what we are calling *geo-propaganda*. Geo-propaganda is defined as the use of digitally gathered location data for political manipulation. After the 2016 Cambridge Analytica scandal, Facebook limited access to its Graph API, the tool that the now-defunct digital consultancy used to gather information on users and their connections.[36] Because of this restriction, political campaigns are scrambling to come up with new ways to gather massive behavioral data sets on people and their networks. These data sets, paired with sophisticated computation and human oversight, can yield useful information about, say, undecided voters or particular demographic groups. That information can be used to target particular groups for propaganda, for example by using location data–generated information to introduce Florida Latinos to conspiracy theories like QAnon.[37] Tools that gather geographic data, from geofencing to Bluetooth beacons, have been used in the commercial sphere for years. These tools can isolate a particular area and gather information on people spending time there. This might seem benign, but what if the digital "fence" is drawn around an abortion clinic or a church? When combined with other data, this location information could be used to manipulate both individuals and groups. In 2020, the conservative group CatholicVote, for instance, gathered geolocation data on U.S. Catholics to get them to vote against candidates who supported abortion rights and gay marriage.[38] Political campaigns, governments, NGOs, lobbying groups, and others have told us they believe they can harness this geolocation information to effectively target political messages to highly specific groups, and political groups are now trying to use geolocation tools to back their way into the Facebook Graph API.

Meanwhile, politicians like Narendra Modi, Donald Trump, and Joe Biden are building their own political social media apps. Supporters can download these apps to get information from the campaigns, volunteer, or engage with likeminded folks; the Trump and Modi apps are also highly gamified (usually intended to make them harder to put down). When my research team dug deeper into these applications, we found that they gathered large amounts of data on users, including the locations of their smart phones and their contacts.[39] The data gathered on these apps can be triangulated with other data on voters, including broader troves of geolocation data, to propagandize more effectively.

To combat geo-propaganda, lawmakers must institute more robust data privacy laws. The EU has led the way with the General Data Protection Regulation, but we need more targeted laws aimed at protecting people's location and behavioral data. We cannot continue to allow chat applications, other third-party apps, and social media to take advantage of people by way of obscure and exhaustingly long terms of service agreements. People must be told, up front and in simple language, how their data will be used. They should always have a right to easily opt out. Regulators around the globe should make it illegal for political groups to gather location data. People may be able to stomach commercial entities' gathering their locations and using that information to sell them products. But no one should accept political organizations' attempts to spy on them to manipulate their opinions.

Some final recommendations and solutions to both old and new problems of computational propaganda have also been triggered by my interviews and fieldwork. While many machine learning experts are worried about the manipulative use of AI, machine learning, and deep learning, others are optimistic about how these automated tools are already being used to detect inorganic informational manipulation. Some social media firms, say interviewees who work there, are using machine learning–driven behavioral analyses to detect small groups' information operations. Other experts told me about new systems for limiting the manipulative use of virtual private networks, which can hide a user's true IP address and geographic location. For instance, new machine learning systems are being purpose-built to make sure people are where they say they are so someone in, say, Saint Petersburg can't pretend online that they are in Texas. Information security experts are cautiously excited about these steps, but they are also quick to point out that, like any other digital technology, they could also be used for nefarious purposes. I wouldn't, for example, want these new location verification tools in the hands of geo-propagandists.

Social media networks built with "zero trust security" are another proposed means of combating manipulation. In such a system, anyone trying to gain entry must first verify their identity. This can prevent hacking; it can also prevent computational propaganda by political actors hoping to remain anonymous. Social media sites like Twitter, which simply require a phone number or e-mail from a new user, are much less secure and much more open to computational propaganda. Zero trust security can be used for ill too, however; sites like Parler, which allow their platforms to be used to spread extremism, white supremacy, and hate, already use these types of "real identity" verification processes. This enables them to access much more sensitive data about their users (such as driver's license numbers, Social Security numbers, or passport images).

Finally, there must be stiff regulations and penalties for creation, promotion, or use of computational propaganda at any level. People who use computational propaganda to attack protected groups, to harass and threaten individuals, and to spread disinformation about voting and political processes must be held criminally liable. Social media companies that allow this content to go viral on their apps and sites should have some significant penalty—not just fines—that remove their incentives to ignore it. In the United States, laws must catch up with the current media landscape. Section 230 of the Communications Decency Act (which was written in 1996) needs to be replaced with legislation that takes account of the massive rise of social media. Platforms must be held liable for information they promote and curate. The Federal Elections Commission, Federal Trade Commission, and Federal Communications Commission must also step up and prevent manipulation via digital tools. None of these agencies has done anything like enough to monitor and prevent computational propaganda and other forms of wrongdoing on social media, where all of these regulators' concerns—political manipulation, commercial manipulation, and mediated manipulation—overlap. Other countries should similarly work to regulate the online sphere, holding bad actors liable while also preserving people's rights to free speech and privacy. This will be tricky to navigate but it must be done.

Progress has been made. Social media companies are stepping up to make bot makers' lives more difficult, and they are beginning to take propaganda more seriously. These are welcome changes, but they are baby steps. These companies still have a lot of work to do. It is the job of lawmakers and reporters—and of regular people like you and me—to continue to hold them accountable. We must have systematic change in the digital landscape—new forms of social media purpose-built to prevent the most harmful propaganda we see today. We have a long way yet to go, but I, for one, am hopeful.

Notes

1. Propaganda, Social Media, and Political Bots

1. As with all interviewees in this book, I've given Hernan a pseudonym.

2. Ryan Broderick and Íñigo Arredondo, "Meet the 29-Year-Old Trying to Become the King of Mexican Fake News," *BuzzFeed News*, June 28, 2018, https://www.buzzfeednews.com/article/ryanhatesthis/meet-the-29-year-old-trying-to-become-the-king-of-mexican.

3. Andrew Rosati and Mario Sergio Lima, "In Hunt for 'Office of Hate,' Brazil's Supreme Court Closes In," *Bloomberg*, June 22, 2020, https://www.bloomberg.com/news/articles/2020-06-22/in-hunt-for-office-of-hate-brazil-s-supreme-court-closes-in.

4. Samuel Woolley, "Manufacturing Consensus: Computational Propaganda and the 2016 U.S. Presidential Election" (PhD diss., University of Washington, 2018).

5. Soroush Vosoughi, Deb Roy, and Sinan Aral, "The Spread of True and False News Online," *Science* 359, no. 6380 (March 9, 2018): 1146–51, https://doi.org/10.1126/science.aap9559.

6. Langdon Winner, *The Whale and the Reactor* (Chicago: University of Chicago Press, 1986), 112.

7. Walter Lippmann, *Public Opinion* (1922; reprint, New York: Simon and Schuster, 1997).

8. Edward L. Bernays, *Propaganda* (1928; reprint, New York: Ig, 2005).

9. Lippmann, *Public Opinion*.

10. Edward S. Herman and Noam Chomsky, *Manufacturing Consent: The Political Economy of the Mass Media* (New York: Pantheon, 2002).

11. Antonio Gramsci, *Selections from Prison Notebooks* (Durham, NC: Duke University Press, 2007).

12. Sandra K. Evans et al., "Explicating Affordances: A Conceptual Framework for Understanding Affordances in Communication Research," *Journal of*

Computer-Mediated Communication 22, no. 1 (2017): 35–52, https://doi.org/10.1111/jcc4.12180.

13. Woolley, "Manufacturing Consensus," 3.

14. This dynamic recalls the spiral of silence, that palpable fear of isolation people feel when realizing they might think differently from those around them. Elisabeth Noelle-Neumann, *The Spiral of Silence: Public Opinion—Our Social Skin* (Chicago: University of Chicago Press, 1993).

15. Jacques Ellul, *Propaganda: The Formation of Men's Attitudes* (New York: Vintage, 1973).

16. Philip N. Howard and Malcolm R. Parks, "Social Media and Political Change: Capacity, Constraint, and Consequence," *Journal of Communication* 62, no. 2 (2012): 359–62, https://doi.org/10.1111/j.1460–2466.2012.01626.

17. Yochai Benkler, Robert Faris, and Hal Roberts, *Network Propaganda: Manipulation, Disinformation, and Radicalization in American Politics* (New York: Oxford University Press, 2018).

18. Whitney Phillips, "The Oxygen of Amplification: Better Practices for Reporting on Extremists, Antagonists, and Manipulators," *Data and Society* (Data and Society Research Institute, May 22, 2018), https://datasociety.net/library/oxygen-of-amplification/.

19. Joan Donovan, "The Lifecycle of Media Manipulation," *DataJournalism.com*, n.d., https://datajournalism.com/read/handbook/verification-3/investigating-disinformation-and-media-manipulation/the-lifecycle-of-media-manipulation.

20. Samuel C. Woolley and Philip N. Howard, "Automation, Algorithms, and Politics: Political Communication, Computational Propaganda, and Autonomous Agents—Introduction," *International Journal of Communication* 10, no. 10 (October 12, 2016): 9.

21. Norah Abokhodair, Daisy Yoo, and David W. McDonald, "Dissecting a Social Botnet: Growth, Content and Influence in Twitter," in *Proceedings of the 18th ACM Conference on Computer Supported Cooperative Work and Social Computing* (New York: Association for Computing Machinery, 2015), 839–51, https://doi.org/10.1145/2675133.2675208.

22. Samuel C. Woolley, "Automating Power: Social Bot Interference in Global Politics," *First Monday* 21, no. 4 (March 10, 2016), https://doi.org/10.5210/fm.v21i4.6161.

23. Philip N. Howard, "Network Ethnography and the Hypermedia Organization: New Media, New Organizations, New Methods," *New Media and Society* 4, no. 4 (June 30, 2016), https://doi.org/10.1177/146144402321466813.

24. Gilad Lotan, "#FreddieGray—Is Not Trending on Twitter?" *Medium*, April 24, 2015, https://medium.com/i-data/freddiegray-is-not-trending-on-twitter -9e4550607a39.

25. J. Ratkiewicz et al., "Detecting and Tracking Political Abuse in Social Media," *Proceedings of the International AAAI Conference on Web and Social Media* 5, no. 1 (2021): 297–304, https://ojs.aaai.org/index.php/ICWSM/article/view/14127.

26. Katie Joseff, Anastasia Goodwin, and Samuel Woolley, "Nanoinfluencers Are Slyly Barnstorming the 2020 Election," *Wired*, August 15, 2020, https://www.wired .com/story/opinion-nanoinfluencers-are-slyly-barnstorming-the-2020-election/.

27. Panagiotis T. Metaxas, Eni Mustafaraj, and Dani Gayo-Avello, "How (Not) to Predict Elections," in *2011 IEEE Third International Conference on Privacy, Security, Risk and Trust and 2011 IEEE Third International Conference on Social Computing* (Boston: IEEE, 2011), 165–71, https://doi.org/10.1109/PASSAT/SocialCom .2011.98.

28. Eni Mustafaraj and Panagiotis T. Metaxas, "What Edited Retweets Reveal about Online Political Discourse," in *Analyzing Microtext: Papers from the 2011 AAAI Workshop* (Palo Alto: AAAI, 2011), 38–43.

29. Marion R. Just et al., "'It's Trending on Twitter'—An Analysis of the Twitter Manipulations in the Massachusetts 2010 Special Senate Election," SSRN Scholarly Paper (Rochester, NY: Social Science Research Network, August 23, 2012), https:// papers.ssrn.com/abstract=2108272.

30. Thomas B. Edsall, "Trump's Digital Advantage Is Freaking Out Democratic Strategists," *New York Times*, January 29, 2020, https://www.nytimes.com/2020/01/ 29/opinion/trump-digital-campaign-2020.html.

31. Kevin Poulsen and Desiderio Andrew, "Russian Hackers' New Target: A Vulnerable Democratic Senator," *Daily Beast*, July 26, 2018, https://www.thedailybeast .com/russian-hackers-new-target-a-vulnerable-democratic-senator.

32. Samuel Woolley, *The Reality Game: How the Next Wave of Technology Will Break the Truth* (New York: PublicAffairs, 2020).

33. Philip N. Howard, *Pax Technica: How the Internet of Things May Set Us Free or Lock Us Up* (New Haven, CT: Yale University Press, 2015).

34. Jeff Orlowski, *The Social Dilemma*, streaming video (Netflix, 2020).

35. Jason Lanier, *Ten Arguments for Deleting Your Social Media Accounts Right Now* (New York: Henry Holt, 2018).

36. Randall Lewis, Justin M. Rao, and David H. Reiley, "Measuring the Effects of Advertising: The Digital Frontier" (Working Paper, National Bureau of Economic Research, October 2013), https://doi.org/10.3386/w19520; Tim Hwang, *Subprime*

Attention Crisis: Advertising and the Time Bomb at the Heart of the Internet (New York: FSG Originals, 2020).

37. Joshua A. Tucker et al., "Social Media, Political Polarization, and Political Disinformation: A Review of the Scientific Literature," Hewlett Foundation, March 19, 2018, https://hewlett.org/library/social-media-political-polarization-political-dis information-review-scientific-literature/.

38. Kathleen Hall Jamieson, *Cyberwar: How Russian Hackers and Trolls Helped Elect a President: What We Don't, Can't, and Do Know* (Oxford: Oxford University Press, 2018).

39. Ellul, *Propaganda.*

40. Nicholas Monaco, Carly Nyst, and Samuel Woolley, "State-Sponsored Trolling: How Governments Are Deploying Disinformation as Part of Broader Digital Harassment Campaigns," Institute for the Future, 2020, https://www.iftf.org/statesponsoredtrolling.

41. Kimberly Grambo, "Fake News and Racial, Ethnic, and Religious Minorities: A Precarious Quest for Truth," *University of Pennsylvania Journal of Constitutional Law* 21, no. 5 (January 1, 2019): 1299.

42. Becca Lewis and Alice E. Marwick, "Media Manipulation and Disinformation Online," *Data and Society* (Data and Society Research Institute, May 15, 2017), https://datasociety.net/library/media-manipulation-and-disinfo-online/.

43. Samuel Woolley and Douglas Guilbeault, "United States: Manufacturing Consensus Online," in *Computational Propaganda: Political Parties, Politicians, and Political Manipulation on Social Media,* ed. Samuel Woolley and Philip Howard (Oxford: Oxford University Press, 2018), 185–212.

44. Disciplines that have struggled to contend with how the rise of the web, writ large, changes their theories and models. See, e.g., Ekaterina Zhuravskaya, Maria Petrova, and Ruben Enikolopov, "Political Effects of the Internet and Social Media," *Annual Review of Economics* 12 (August 2020): 415–38.

45. Kate Starbird, Twitter post, October 9, 2019, https://twitter.com/katestarbird/status/1182093465603039232.

46. Caroline Jack, "Lexicon of Lies," *Data and Society* (Data and Society Research Institute, August 9, 2017), https://datasociety.net/library/lexicon-of-lies/.

47. "The Next Campaign Text You Get May Be from a Friend," *Wired*, January 2, 2020, https://www.wired.com/story/relational-organizing-apps-2020-campaign/.

48. Robert S. Mueller, *Report on the Investigation into Russian Interference in the 2016 Presidential Election* (Washington, DC: U.S. Department of Justice, 2019), https://www.justice.gov/storage/report.pdf.

49. Shelby Grossman, Daniel Bush, and Renee DiResta, "Evidence of Russia-Linked Influence Operations in Africa," Stanford Internet Observatory, October 29, 2019, https://fsi.stanford.edu/news/prigozhin-africa.

50. Nicholas Monaco, Melanie Smith, and Amy Studdart, "Detecting Digital Fingerprints: Tracing Chinese Disinformation in Taiwan," Graphika, 2020, https://graphika.com/reports/detecting-digital-fingerprints-tracing-chinese-disinformation-in-taiwan/; William M. Arkin, "As Tensions Rose, U.S. Intelligence Spotted Election Meddling by China, Russia, Iran," *Newsweek,* November 8, 2021, https://www.newsweek.com/tensions-rose-us-intelligence-spotted-election-meddling-china-russia-iran-1646722.

51. Taberez Ahmed Neyazi, "Digital Propaganda, Political Bots and Polarized Politics in India," *Asian Journal of Communication* 30, no. 1 (January 2, 2020): 39–57, https://doi.org/10.1080/01292986.2019.1699938.

52. Gabriel Pereira, Iago Bojczuk, and Lisa Parks, "WhatsApp Disruptions in Brazil: A Content Analysis of User and News Media Responses, 2015–2018," preprint, MediArXiv, May 4, 2020, https://doi.org/10.33767/osf.io/k2hjv.

53. Aim Sinpeng, Dimitar Gueorguiev, and Aries A. Arugay, "Strong Fans, Weak Campaigns: Social Media and Duterte in the 2016 Philippine Election," *Journal of East Asian Studies* 20, no. 3 (2020): 1–22, https://doi.org/10.1017/jea.2020.11.

54. "Social Media Propelled Ethnocentric Disinformation and Propaganda During the Nigerian Elections," Global Voices Advox, November 6, 2019, https://advox.globalvoices.org/2019/11/06/social-media-propelled-ethnocentric-disinformation-and-propaganda-during-the-nigerian-elections/.

55. Erkan Saka, "Social Media in Turkey as a Space for Political Battles: AKTrolls and Other Politically Motivated Trolling," *Middle East Critique* 27, no. 2 (April 3, 2018): 161–77, https://doi.org/10.1080/19436149.2018.1439271.

56. Samuel Woolley et al., "The Bot Proxy: Designing Automated Self Expression," in *A Networked Self and Platforms, Stories, Connections,* ed. Zizi Papacharissi (New York: Routledge, 2018), 59–76.

57. Yazan Boshmaf et al., "The Socialbot Network: When Bots Socialize for Fame and Money," in *Proceedings of the 27th Annual Computer Security Applications Conference* (New York: Association for Computing Machinery, 2011), 93–102, https://doi.org/10.1145/2076732.2076746.

58. Benkler, Faris, and Roberts, *Network Propaganda,* 25.

59. Alex Stamos, "An Update on Information Operations on Facebook," About, Meta, September 6, 2017, https://about.fb.com/news/2017/09/information-operations-update/.

60. Shadab Nazmi, Dhruv Nenwani, and Gagan Narhe, "Social Media Rumours in India: Counting the Dead," *BBC News,* 2018, https://www.bbc.co.uk/news/resources/idt-e5043092-f7f0-42e9-9848-5274ac896e6d.

61. Paul Mozur, "A Genocide Incited on Facebook, with Posts from Myanmar's Military," *New York Times,* October 15, 2018, https://www.nytimes.com/2018/10/15/technology/myanmar-facebook-genocide.html.

62. Monaco, Nyst, and Woolley, "State-Sponsored Trolling."

63. Josephine Lukito et al., "The Wolves in Sheep's Clothing: How Russia's Internet Research Agency Tweets Appeared in U.S. News as Vox Populi," *International Journal of Press/Politics* 25, no. 2 (April 1, 2020): 196–216, https://doi.org/10.1177/1940161219895215.

64. Jennifer Alejandro, "Journalism in the Age of Social Media," Reuters Institute for the Study of Journalism, 2010, https://reutersinstitute.politics.ox.ac.uk/our-research/journalism-age-social-media.

65. Frederick Schauer, "Fear, Risk and the First Amendment: Unraveling the Chilling Effect," *Boston University Law Review* 58, no. 5 (1978): 685–732.

2. Understanding Manufactured Consensus

1. Harold D. Lasswell, "The Theory of Political Propaganda," *American Political Science Review* 21 (1927): 631.

2. Vindu Goel, Suhasini Raj, and Priyadarshini Ravichandran, "How Whats-App Leads Mobs to Murder in India," *New York Times,* July 18, 2018, https://www.nytimes.com/interactive/2018/07/18/technology/whatsapp-india-killings.html; Timothy McLaughlin, "How WhatsApp Fuels Fake News and Violence in India," *Wired,* December 12, 2010, https://www.wired.com/story/how-whatsapp-fuels-fake-news-and-violence-in-india/; Mohammad Ali, "The Rise of a Hindu Vigilante in the Age of WhatsApp and Modi," *Wired,* April 14, 2020, https://www.wired.com/story/indias-frightening-descent-social-media-terror/.

3. Russel Mindich, "The Future of Organizing Is Relational," *Medium,* June 25, 2020, https://medium.com/outvote/the-future-of-organizing-is-relational-a435fb6e1a4c.

4. Walter Lippmann, *Public Opinion* (1922; reprint, New York: Simon and Schuster, 1997).

5. Harold D. Lasswell, *Propaganda Technique in the World War* (PhD diss., University of Chicago, 1926).

6. Edward L. Bernays, *Propaganda* (1928; reprint, New York: Ig, 2005).

7. Jacques Ellul, *Propaganda: The Formation of Men's Attitudes* (New York: Vintage, 1973).

8. Edward S. Herman and Noam Chomsky, *Manufacturing Consent: The Political Economy of the Mass Media* (New York: Pantheon, 2002).

9. Garth S. Jowett and Victoria J. O'Donnell, *Propaganda and Persuasion*, 5th ed. (Thousand Oaks, CA: SAGE, 2011).

10. Stanley B. Cunningham, *The Idea of Propaganda: A Reconstruction* (Westport, CT: Greenwood, 2002).

11. Michael Schudson, "The 'Lippmann-Dewey Debate' and the Invention of Walter Lippmann as an Anti-Democrat, 1985–1996," *International Journal of Communication* 2, no. 12 (September 22, 2008): 1031–42.

12. Ellul, *Propaganda*.

13. Bernays, *Propaganda*, 10.

14. Ibid., 9.

15. Literally "good" + "message" + "-ism." "Ev-" is just a form of "eu-," the Greek root for "good" (euphonia, euphoria, eustress, eugenics, etc.). "Angel" means message.

16. Lippmann, *Public Opinion*; Bernays, *Propaganda*.

17. Reluctantly in the case of Lippman, wholeheartedly when it came to Bernays.

18. Edward L. Bernays, "The Engineering of Consent," *Annals of the American Academy of Political and Social Science* 250, no. 1 (1947): 113–20, https://doi.org/10.1177/000271624725000116.

19. Harold D. Lasswell, "Propaganda Technique in the World War" (PhD diss., University of Chicago, 1926).

20. Ellul, *Propaganda*.

21. Ibid., v.

22. Yochai Benkler, Robert Faris, and Hal Roberts, *Network Propaganda: Manipulation, Disinformation, and Radicalization in American Politics* (New York: Oxford University Press, 2018).

23. Sallie Hughes and Chappell Lawson, "Propaganda and Crony Capitalism: Partisan Bias in Mexican Television News," *Latin American Research Review* 39, no. 3 (2004): 81–105, https://www.researchgate.net/publication/236820305_Propaganda_and_Crony_Capitalism_Partisan_Bias_in_Mexican_Television_News.

24. Marcel H. Van Herpen, *Putin's Propaganda Machine: Soft Power and Russian Foreign Policy* (Lanham, MD: Rowman and Littlefield, 2015).

25. Elda Brogi et al., "Assessing Certain Recent Developments in the Hungarian Media Market Through the Prism of the Media Pluralism Monitor," European University Institute, 2019, https://www.doi.org/10.2870/560715.

26. Benkler, Faris, and Roberts, *Network Propaganda,* 28.

27. Jowett and O'Donnell, *Propaganda and Persuasion.*

28. Ellul, *Propaganda,* xii.

29. Ibid.

30. A version of this concept, in the form of "engineering assent," is also key to the Marxist theorization of Antonio Gramsci, who posited it as a tool of control that the dominant exercised over the subjugated class. Gramsci, *Prison Notebooks* (New York: Columbia University Press, 1992).

31. Lippmann, *Public Opinion,* 69. Lippmann himself was one.

32. Ibid., 21; Graham Wallas, *Human Nature in Politics* (London: A. Constable, 1908); Charles-Marie Gustave Le Bon, *The Crowd: A Study of the Popular Mind* (London: T. F. Unwin, 1897).

33. Lippmann, *Public Opinion,* 6, 8.

34. Bernays, *The Engineering of Consent.*

35. Edward L. Bernays, *Crystallizing Public Opinion* (New York: Boni and Liveright, 1923), 10.

36. Ibid., 138.

37. Bernays, *Propaganda,* 9.

38. Ellul, *Propaganda,* viii, x.

39. Herman and Chomsky, *Manufacturing Consent,* xi.

40. Ibid., xii.

41. Ibid., xv, xvi.

42. Larry Diamond, "Liberation Technology," *Journal of Democracy* 21, no. 3 (July 14, 2010): 69–83, https://doi.org/10.1353/jod.0.0190.

43. Evgeny Morozov, *The Net Delusion: The Dark Side of Internet Freedom* (Cambridge, MA: Perseus Books, 2011).

44. Herman and Chomsky, *Manufacturing Consent,* 3.

45. Ibid., 4.

46. Siva Vaidhyanathan, *The Googlization of Everything (And Why We Should Worry)* (Berkeley: University of California Press, 2012); Steven Levy, *Facebook: The Inside Story* (New York: Blue Rider Press, 2020).

47. Herman and Chomsky, *Manufacturing Consent,* 14.

48. Marcel Broersma and Todd Graham, "Social Media as Beat," *Journalism Practice* 6, no. 3 (June 1, 2012): 403–19, https://doi.org/10.1080/17512786.2012.663626;

Frank Esser and Michael Brüggemann, "The Strategic Crisis of German Newspapers," in *The Changing Business of Journalism and Its Implications for Democracy,* ed. David A. L. Levy and Rasmus Kleis Nielsen (Oxford: Reuters Institute, 2020), 39–54.

49. Although social media firms have made a legal argument that they "aren't media companies," the easy fit of their inclusion alongside the traditional mass media firms discussed in the first and second filters should suggest otherwise.

50. Herman and Chomsky, *Manufacturing Consensus,* 18.

51. Safiya Umoja Noble, *Algorithms of Oppression: How Search Engines Reinforce Racism* (New York: NYU Press, 2018); Cathy O'Neil, *Weapons of Math Destruction: How Big Data Increases Inequality and Threatens Democracy* (New York: Crown, 2016).

52. Herman and Chomsky, *Manufacturing Consensus,* 26.

53. Suzanne Vranica and Deepa Seetharaman, "Facebook Tightens Controls on Speech as Ad Boycott Grows," *Wall Street Journal,* June 27, 2020, https://www.wsj.com/articles/unilever-to-halt-u-s-ads-on-facebook-and-twitter-for-rest-of-2020-11593187230.

54. Simon Kemp, "India Overtakes the USA to Become Facebook's #1 Country," The Next Web, July 13, 2017, https://thenextweb.com/contributors/2017/07/13/india-overtakes-usa-become-facebooks-top-country/.

55. Billy Perrigo, "Facebook's Ties to India's Ruling Party Complicate Its Fight Against Hate Speech," *Time,* August 27, 2020, https://time.com/5883993/india-facebook-hate-speech-bjp/.

56. Patricia Mazzei and Jennifer Medina, "False Political News in Spanish Pits Latino Voters Against Black Lives Matter," *New York Times,* October 21, 2020, https://www.nytimes.com/2020/10/21/us/politics/spanish-election-2020-disinformation.html.

57. Robert S. Mueller, *Report on the Investigation into Russian Interference in the 2016 Presidential Election* (Washington, DC: U.S. Department of Justice, 2019), https://www.justice.gov/storage/report.pdf; Vidya Narayanan et al., "Russian Involvement and Junk News During Brexit," The Computational Propaganda Project: Algorithms, Automation and Digital Politics, 2017, https://comprop.oii.ox.ac.uk/research/working-papers/Russia-and-brexit; Alina Polyakova, "The Kremlin's Plot Against Democracy: How Russia Updated Its 2016 Playbook for 2020 Essays," *Foreign Affairs* 99, no. 5 (2020): 140–49; Lara Jakes, "As Protests in South America Surged, So Did Russian Trolls on Twitter, U.S. Finds," *New York Times,* January 20, 2020, https://www.nytimes.com/2020/01/19/us/politics/south-america-russian-twitter.html.

58. Jim Rutenberg, "RT, Sputnik and Russia's New Theory of War," *New York Times*, September 13, 2017, https://www.nytimes.com/2017/09/13/magazine/rt -sputnik-and-russias-new-theory-of-war.html; Robert McMillan, "Twitter Takes Down Chinese Government-Linked Accounts It Says Pushed Propaganda," *Wall Street Journal*, June 11, 2020, https://www.wsj.com/articles/twitter-takes-down -chinese-government-linked-accounts-it-says-pushed-propaganda-11591909280; Nicholas Monaco, Melanie Smith, and Amy Studdart, "Detecting Digital Finger- prints: Tracing Chinese Disinformation in Taiwan," Graphika, 2020, https:// graphika.com/reports/detecting-digital-fingerprints-tracing-chinese-disinformation -in-taiwan/; "Free Tibet Exposes #ChinaSpam on Twitter," Free Tibet, July 17, 2014, https://freetibet.org/news-media/na/free-tibet-exposes-chinaspam-twitter; Jeff Kao, Mia Shuang Li, "How China Built a Twitter Propaganda Machine Then Let It Loose on Coronavirus," ProPublica, March 26, 2020, https://www.propublica.org/article/ how-china-built-a-twitter-propaganda-machine-then-let-it-loose-on-coronavirus.

59. Kimberly A. Powell, "Framing Islam: An Analysis of U.S. Media Coverage of Terrorism Since 9/11," *Communication Studies* 62, no. 1 (January 31, 2011): 90–112, https://doi.org/10.1080/10510974.2011.533599.

60. Joshua A. Tucker et al., "Social Media, Political Polarization, and Politi- cal Disinformation: A Review of the Scientific Literature," Hewlett Foundation, March 19, 2018, https://hewlett.org/library/social-media-political-polarization -political-disinformation-review-scientific-literature/.

61. John-Paul Verkamp and Minaxi Gupta, "Five Incidents, One Theme: Twitter Spam as a Weapon to Drown Voices of Protest," paper presented at the USENIX Workshop on Free and Open Communications on the Internet (FOCI), Washing- ton, DC, August 13, 2013.

62. Samuel Woolley, "#HackingTeam Leaks: Ecuador Is Spending Millions on Malware, Pro-Government Trolls," Global Voices Advox, August 4, 2015, https://advox.globalvoices.org/2015/08/04/hackingteam-leaks-ecuador-is-spending -millions-on-malware-pro-government-trolls/.

63. Samantha Bradshaw and Philip N. Howard, "Troops, Trolls and Trouble- makers: A Global Inventory of Organized Social Media Manipulation," in *Project on Computational Propaganda*, ed. Samuel Woolley and Philip N. Howard (Ox- ford: Oxford Internet Institute, 2017), https://demtech.oii.ox.ac.uk/research/posts/ troops-trolls-and-troublemakers-a-global-inventory-of-organized-social-media -manipulation.

64. Dan Arnaudo, "Computational Propaganda in Brazil: Social Bots during Elec- tions," in *Project on Computational Propaganda*, ed. Samuel Woolley and Philip N.

Howard (Oxford: Oxford Internet Institute, 2017), https://demtech.oii.ox.ac.uk/research/posts/computational-propaganda-in-brazil-social-bots-during-elections/.

65. Samuel Woolley, "Manufacturing Consensus: Computational Propaganda and the 2016 U.S. Presidential Election" (PhD diss., University of Washington, 2018).

66. Farhad Manjoo, "How Twitter Is Being Gamed to Feed Misinformation," *New York Times*, May 31, 2017, https://www.nytimes.com/2017/05/31/technology/how-twitter-is-being-gamed-to-feed-misinformation.html.

67. K. Tanaka, "The Threat of Computational Propaganda," *Nightly News*, July 20, 2017, http://www3.nhk.or.jp/news/web_tokushu/2017_0720.html?utm_int=news_content.

68. Bridget Coyne, "How #Election2016 Was Tweeted So Far," Twitter (blog), November 7, 2017, https://blog.twitter.com/official/en_us/a/2016/how-election2016-was-tweeted-so-far.html.

69. Erika Franklin Fowler, Travis N. Ridout, and Michael M. Franz, "Political Advertising in 2016: The Presidential Election as Outlier?" *Forum* 14, no. 4 (December 1, 2016): 445–69, https://doi.org/10.1515/for-2016–0040.

70. Dipayan Ghosh and Ben Scott, "Facebook's New Controversy Shows How Easily Online Political Ads Can Manipulate You," *Time*, March 19, 2018, https://time.com/5197255/facebook-cambridge-analytica-donald-trump-ads-data/.

71. B. Kollanyi, P. N. Howard, and S. C. Woolley, *Bots and Automation over Twitter during the U.S. Election* (Oxford: Project on Computational Propaganda, 2016), 5, http://www.politicalbots.org; Alessandro Bessi and Emilio Ferrara, "Social Bots Distort the 2016 U.S. Presidential Election Online Discussion," *First Monday* 21, no. 11 (November 3, 2016), https://doi.org/10.5210/fm.v21i11.7090.

72. C. Bialik, "Everyone Has Fake Twitter Followers, but Trump Has the Most. Sad!" FiveThirtyEight, April 14, 2016, https://fivethirtyeight.com/features/everyone-has-fake-twitter-followers-but-trump-has-the-most-sad/.

73. Nick Bilton, "Trump's Biggest Lie? The Size of His Twitter Following," *Vanity Fair*, August 4, 2016, https://www.vanityfair.com/news/2016/08/trumps-biggest-lie-the-size-of-his-twitter-following.

74. Daniel Kreiss, *Prototype Politics: Technology-Intensive Campaigning and the Data of Democracy* (New York: Oxford University Press, 2016), 3.

3. State Use of Computational Propaganda

1. Irene Caselli, "Assessing Correa's Free Speech Heritage," *Index on Censorship* 45, no. 4 (December 1, 2016): 83–86, https://doi.org/10.1177/0306422016685995;

"Ecuador's Rafael Correa Under Fire for Media Laws," *BBC News*, February 2, 2012, https://www.bbc.com/news/world-latin-america-16806224.

2. He was tried in absentia; he now lives in Belgium.

3. Samuel Woolley, "#HackingTeam Leaks: Ecuador Is Spending Millions on Malware, Pro-Government Trolls," Global Voices Advox, August 4, 2015, https://advox.globalvoices.org/2015/08/04/hackingteam-leaks-ecuador-is-spending-millions-on-malware-pro-government-trolls/.

4. Ibid.

5. Ibid.

6. Jillian C. York, "Syria's Twitter Spambots," *Guardian*, April 21, 2011, https://www.theguardian.com/commentisfree/2011/apr/21/syria-twitter-spambots-pro-revolution.

7. Anas Qtiesh, "Spam Bots Flooding Twitter to Drown Info About #Syria Protests," Global Voices Advox, April 18, 2011, http://www.anasqtiesh.com/2011/04/spam-bots-flooding-twitter-to-drown-info-about-syria-protests/.

8. Norah Abokhodair, Daisy Yoo, and David W. McDonald, "Dissecting a Social Botnet: Growth, Content and Influence in Twitter," in *Proceedings of the 18th ACM Conference on Computer Supported Cooperative Work and Social Computing—CSCW '15* (New York: Association for Computing Machinery, 2015), 839–51, https://doi.org/10.1145/2675133.2675208.

9. Samuel C. Woolley, "Automating Power: Social Bot Interference in Global Politics," *First Monday* 21, no. 4 (March 10, 2016), https://doi.org/10.5210/fm.v21i4.6161.

10. Samantha Bradshaw and Philip N. Howard, *The Global Disinformation Order: 2019 Global Inventory of Organised Social Media Manipulation* (Oxford: Project on Computational Propaganda, 2019), i, 1; Samantha Bradshaw and Philip N. Howard, "Challenging Truth and Trust: A Global Inventory of Organized Social Media Manipulation," *Computational Propaganda Project* 1 (2018), https://demtech.oii.ox.ac.uk/wp-content/uploads/sites/93/2018/07/ct2018.pdf; Samantha Bradshaw and Philip N. Howard, "Troops, Trolls and Troublemakers: A Global Inventory of Organized Social Media Manipulation," in *Project on Computational Propaganda*, ed. Samuel Woolley and Philip N. Howard (Oxford: Oxford Internet Institute, 2017), https://demtech.oii.ox.ac.uk/research/posts/troops-trolls-and-troublemakers-a-global-inventory-of-organized-social-media-manipulation.

11. As I dived deeper into my own research on computational propaganda, I began to realize that the problem wasn't just states and their constituent parts. My colleagues and I, as well as other researchers, found early examples of nonstate-based

actors' use of computational propaganda or "online astroturfing." We also found evidence that other powerful political actors—corporations, candidates for office, and even NGOs—were using social media bots and sockpuppet accounts in efforts to support their own causes on social media. Many of these users were well-resourced and had tangible connections to state governments, and they were able to wage sophisticated campaigns.

12. Nicholas Monaco, Carly Nyst, and Samuel Woolley, "State-Sponsored Trolling: How Governments Are Deploying Disinformation as Part of Broader Digital Harassment Campaigns," Institute for the Future, July 19, 2018, https://www.iftf .org/statesponsoredtrolling.

13. The original state-sponsored trolling report was "a collective effort involving a number of people who have been active in developing this field of research and directed by Camille Francois. The original methodology for this research was developed by Francois, Javier Luque, Ellery Biddle, and Ivan Sigal, with additional input from a number of Global Voices and International Press Institute contributors. Much of the original research for the paper was also contributed by Marianne Diaz, Gülsin Harman, Dağhan Irak, Simin Kagar, and other affiliates of Global Voices and IPI." Ibid. I edited and released the report through my research lab at the Institute for the Future.

14. Mariia Zhdanova and Dariya Orlova, "Computational Propaganda in Ukraine: Caught Between External Threats and Internal Challenges" (Oxford University Computational Propaganda Project Working Paper Series, No. 2017.9, Oxford, UK, 2017), https://demtech.oii.ox.ac.uk/wp-content/uploads/sites/89/2017/ 06/Comprop-Ukraine.pdf.

15. Philip N. Howard, "Hungary's Crackdown on the Press," *New York Times*, September 9, 2014, https://www.nytimes.com/2014/09/09/opinion/hungarys -crackdown-on-the-press.html.

16. Ayla Albayrak and Joe Parkinson, "Turkey's Government Forms 6,000-Member Social Media Team," *Wall Street Journal*, September 16, 2013, https://online.wsj.com/ article/SB10001424127887323527004579079151479634742.html.

17. Jessica McKenzie, "Think Erdogan Will Delete His 18K Strong Twitter Bot Army in Quest to Wipe Out Twitter?" *TechPresident*, March 27, 2014, https://web .archive.org/web/20140330023756/http://techpresident.com/news/wegov/24867/ think-erdogan-will-delete-his-18k-strong-twitter-bot-army-quest-wipe-out-twitter; Erkan Saka, "Social Media in Turkey as a Space for Political Battles: AKTrolls and Other Politically Motivated Trolling," *Middle East Critique* 27, no. 2 (April 3, 2018): 161–77, https://doi.org/10.1080/19436149.2018.1439271.

18. Elcin Poyrazlar, "Turkey's Leader Bans His Own Twitter Bot Army," *Vocativ*, March 26, 2014, https://www.vocativ.com/world/turkey-world/turkeys-leader-nearly-banned-twitter-bot-army/.

19. Emre Kizilkaya, "AKP's Social Media Wars," *Al-Monitor*, November 15, 2013, https://www.al-monitor.com/pulse/originals/2013/11/akp-social-media-twitter-facebook.html; "Turkish PM Accuses 'Robot Lobby' of Conducting Plot Against the Gov't," *Hürriyet Daily News*, February 25, 2014, https://www.hurriyetdailynews.com/turkish-pm-accuses-robot-lobby-of-conducting-plot-against-the-govt-62928.

20. Monaco, Nyst, and Woolley, "State-Sponsored Trolling."

21. Jordan Robertson, Michael Riley, and Andrew Willis, "How to Hack an Election," *Bloomberg*, March 31, 2016, https://www.bloomberg.com/features/2016-how-to-hack-an-election/.

22. Monaco, Nyst, and Woolley, "State-Sponsored Trolling."

23. Ibid., 20.

24. Noam Lupu, Mariana V. Ramírez Bustamante, and Elizabeth J. Zechmeister, "Social Media Disruption: Messaging Mistrust in Latin America," *Journal of Democracy* 31, no. 3 (July 14, 2020): 160–71, https://doi.org/10.1353/jod.2020.0038; Monaco, Nyst, and Woolley, "State-Sponsored Trolling," 19.

25. Yochai Benkler, Robert Faris, and Hal Roberts, *Network Propaganda: Manipulation, Disinformation, and Radicalization in American Politics* (New York: Oxford University Press, 2018).

26. Michael M. Grynbaum, "One America News, the Network That Spreads Conspiracies to the West Wing," *New York Times*, June 9, 2020, https://www.nytimes.com/article/oann-trump.html.

27. Adam Cancryn, "Pro-Jeb Strategist: 'Data Died Tonight,'" *Politico*, November 9, 2016, https://www.politico.com/story/2016/11/mike-murphy-2016-presidential-election-results-231037.

28. "Nate Silver Says Conventional Wisdom, Not Data, Killed 2016 Election Forecasts," *Harvard Gazette*, March 30, 2017, https://news.harvard.edu/gazette/story/2017/03/nate-silver-says-conventional-wisdom-not-data-killed-2016-election-forecasts/.

29. Astead W. Herdon, "Alexandria Ocasio-Cortez on Biden's Win, House Losses, and What's Next for the Left," *New York Times*, November 7, 2020, https://www.nytimes.com/2020/11/07/us/politics/aoc-biden-progressives.html.

30. Kareem Darwish, Walid Magdy, and Tahar Zanouda, "Trump vs. Hillary: What Went Viral During the 2016 US Presidential Election," in *Social Informatics*, ed. Giovanni Luca Ciampaglia, Afra Mashhadi, and Taha Yasseri (Cham, Switzer-

land: Springer International, 2017), 143–61, https://doi.org/10.1007/978-3-319-67217 -5_10.

31. Y. Wang et al., "To Follow or Not to Follow: Analyzing the Growth Patterns of the Trumpists on Twitter," *Proceedings of the International AAAI Conference on Web and Social Media* 10, no. 2 (March 27, 2016): 114–17.

32. Ed Pilkington, "Trump Heaps Praise on Twitter and Denies Using It to Spread Falsehoods," *Guardian*, March 16, 2017, https://www.theguardian.com/us -news/2017/mar/15/donald-trump-twitter-fox-news-interview-wiretapping.

33. Wang et al., "To Follow or Not to Follow."

34. Brian Stelter, "Donald Trump's Twitter Milestone: 20 Million Followers," *CNNMoney*, January 16, 2017, https://money.cnn.com/2017/01/16/media/donald -trump-twitter-20-million-followers/index.html.

35. Ibid.; Alessandro Bessi and Emilio Ferrara, "Social Bots Distort the 2016 U.S. Presidential Election Online Discussion," *First Monday* 21, no. 11 (November 3, 2016), https://doi.org/10.5210/fm.v21i11.7090.

36. Carl Bialik, "Everyone Has Fake Twitter Followers, but Trump Has the Most. Sad!" FiveThirtyEight, April 14, 2016, https://fivethirtyeight.com/features/everyone -has-fake-twitter-followers-but-trump-has-the-most-sad/.

37. Cory L. Armstrong and Fangfang Gao, "Now Tweet This: How News Organizations Use Twitter," *Electronic News*, November 19, 2010, https://doi.org/10.1177/ 1931243110389457; Farida Vis, "Twitter as a Reporting Tool for Breaking News," *Digital Journalism* 1, no. 1 (February 1, 2013): 27–47, https://doi.org/10.1080/21670811 .2012.741316.

38. Chris Wells et al., "Trump, Twitter, and News Media Responsiveness: A Media Systems Approach," *New Media and Society* 22, no. 4 (April 1, 2020): 659–82, https://doi.org/10.1177/1461444819893987.

39. Samuel Woolley and Douglas Guilbeault, "Computational Propaganda in the United States of America: Manufacturing Consensus Online" (Oxford University Computational Propaganda Project Working Paper Series, No. 2017.5, Oxford, UK, 2017), https://blogs.oii.ox.ac.uk/politicalbots/wp-content/uploads/sites/89/2017/ 06/Comprop-USA.pdf.

40. Guido Caldarelli et al., "The Role of Bot Squads in the Political Propaganda on Twitter," *Communications Physics* 3, no. 1 (May 11, 2020): 1–15, https://doi.org/10 .1038/s42005-020-0340-4.

41. Josephine Lukito et al., "The Wolves in Sheep's Clothing: How Russia's Internet Research Agency Tweets Appeared in U.S. News as Vox Populi," *International*

Journal of Press/Politics 25, no. 2 (April 1, 2020): 196–216, https://doi.org/10.1177/1940161219895215.

42. Douglas Guilbeault and Samuel Woolley, "How Twitter Bots Are Shaping the Election," *Atlantic*, November 1, 2016, https://www.theatlantic.com/technology/archive/2016/11/election-bots/506072/; Jim Edwards, "Trump Has Quoted Twitter Bots 150 Times, According to This Analysis of His Tweets," *Business Insider*, April 11, 2016, https://www.businessinsider.com/donald-trump-quote-bots-twitter-2016-4.

43. Benkler, Faris, and Roberts, *Network Propaganda*.

4. Automated Political Influencers

1. "Hungarian PM Sees Shift to Illiberal Christian Democracy in 2019 European Vote," Reuters, July 28, 2018, https://www.reuters.com/article/us-hungary-orban-idUSKBN1KI0BK.

2. Samantha Bradshaw and Philip N. Howard, *The Global Disinformation Order: 2019 Global Inventory of Organised Social Media Manipulation* (Oxford: Project on Computational Propaganda, 2019).

3. Yochai Benkler, Robert Faris, and Hal Roberts, *Network Propaganda: Manipulation, Disinformation, and Radicalization in American Politics* (New York: Oxford University Press, 2018).

4. For example, Yochai Benkler and colleagues also focus on the internet-as-network, titling two books after it. Benkler, *The Wealth of Networks: How Social Production Transforms Markets and Freedom* (New Haven, CT: Yale University Press, 2007); Benkler, Faris, and Roberts, *Network Propaganda*.

5. Philip N. Howard, *The Digital Origins of Dictatorship and Democracy: Information Technology and Political Islam* (Oxford: Oxford University Press, 2010). See also Benkler, *Wealth of Networks*.

6. Zi Chu et al., "Detecting Automation of Twitter Accounts: Are You a Human, Bot, or Cyborg?" *IEEE Transactions on Dependable and Secure Computing* 9, no. 6 (November 2012): 811–24, https://doi.org/10.1109/TDSC.2012.75; David Klepper, "Cyborgs, Trolls and Bots: A Guide to Online Misinformation," AP News, February 7, 2020, https://apnews.com/article/4086949d878336f8ea6daa4dee725d94.

7. A. B. Seligman, *The Idea of Civil Society* (Princeton, NJ: Princeton University Press, 1995).

8. Samuel Woolley et al., "The Bot Proxy: Designing Automated Self Expression," in *A Networked Self and Platforms, Stories, Connections*, ed. Zizi Papacharissi (New York: Routledge, 2018), 59–76.

9. Gina Neff and Peter Nagy, "Talking to Bots: Symbiotic Agency and the Case of Tay," *International Journal of Communication* 10, no. 17 (2016): 4915–31.

10. @DFRLab, "#InfluenceForSale: Venezuela's Twitter Propaganda Mill," *Medium*, February 4, 2019, https://medium.com/dfrlab/influenceforsale-venezuelas -twitter-propaganda-mill-cd20ee4b33d8.

11. Robert Gorwa, *Computational Propaganda in Poland: False Amplifiers and the Digital Public Sphere* (Oxford: Project on Computational Propaganda, 2017).

12. Katie Joseff, Anastasia Goodwin, and Samuel Woolley, "Nanoinfluencers Are Slyly Barnstorming the 2020 Election," *Wired*, 2020, https://www.wired.com/story/ opinion-nanoinfluencers-are-slyly-barnstorming-the-2020-election/.

13. "How Wannabe Instagram Influencers Use Bots to Appear Popular," *Digiday*, August 1, 2017, https://digiday.com/marketing/wannabe-instagram-influencers-use -bots-appear-popular/; Emma Grey Ellis, "Fighting Instagram's $1.3 Billion Problem—Fake Followers," *Wired*, September 10, 2020, https://www.wired.com/story/ instagram-fake-followers/.

14. Alan Cooper, *The Inmates Are Running the Asylum: Why High-Tech Products Drive Us Crazy and How to Restore the Sanity* (Indianapolis: Sams–Pearson Education, 2004).

15. Ian Bogost, *Alien Phenomenology* (Minneapolis: University of Minnesota Press, 2012).

16. Woolley et al., "The Bot Proxy."

17. John Frank Weaver, "Who's Responsible When a Twitter Bot Sends a Threatening Tweet?" *Slate*, February 25, 2015, https://slate.com/technology/2015/02/who-is -responsible-for-death-threats-from-a-twitter-bot.html.

18. Scott Pelley, "How Fake News Becomes a Popular, Trending Topic," *CBS News*, March 26, 2017, https://www.cbsnews.com/news/how-fake-news-find-your -social-media-feeds/.

19. Of course, similar types of efforts do happen on Twitter also, despite the differences in platform architecture and user expectations. An investigative article covered a similar, wholly human-run method of seeding and spreading content over Twitter. This activity occurred in "pro-Trump 'rooms,' private spaces on conservative Twitter that allow followers to coordinate messages and then retweet each other—dramatically multiplying their impact." In these circumstances the goal was to more organically spread provocative political content without seemingly making use of bots. Rather, "manual tweeting is the cardinal rule" because this better took advantage of the "mechanics of attention" set up by platform algorithms. See Shawn Musgrave, "I Get Called a Russian Bot 50 Times a Day," *Politico*, August 9, 2017,

https://www.politico.com/magazine/story/2017/08/09/twitter-trump-train-maga
-echo-chamber-215470.

5. Social Media Companies, the
Technology Industry, and Propaganda

1. Shoshana Zuboff, *The Age of Surveillance Capitalism: The Fight for a Human Future at the New Frontier of Power* (New York: PublicAffairs, 2019).

2. This is unsurprising, given that social media is built on the media advertising structure which grew out of the work of propaganda evangelists like Edward L. Bernays. Bernays, *Propaganda* (1928; reprint, New York: Ig, 2005).

3. See, for instance, Trevor J. Pinch and Wiebe E. Bijker, "The Social Construction of Facts and Artefacts; or, How the Sociology of Science and the Sociology of Technology Might Benefit Each Other," *Social Studies of Science* 14, no. 3 (August 1, 1984): 399–441, https://doi.org/10.1177/030631284014003004, and Lucy A. Suchman, *Plans and Situated Actions: The Problem of Human-Machine Communication*, 2nd ed. (1985; Cambridge: Cambridge University Press, 1987).

4. I say this with deliberate irony. Computers are premised on code that can result in all sorts of different kinds of output, with small changes producing very different outcomes. But the ability to make these changes still lies in the hands of the engineers that maintain the software. The tools are problematic, but so are the actions of the people that build them.

5. Tarleton Gillespie, "The Relevance of Algorithms," in *Media Technologies: Essays on Communication, Materiality, and Society,* ed. Tarleton Gillespie, Pablo J. Boczkowski, and Kirsten A. Foot (Cambridge, MA: MIT Press, 2014), 167.

6. Safiya Umoja Noble, *Algorithms of Oppression: How Search Engines Reinforce Racism* (New York: NYU Press, 2018).

7. Siva Vaidhyanathan, *Antisocial Media: How Facebook Disconnects Us and Undermines Democracy* (New York: Oxford University Press, 2018).

8. Not to be confused with the 2013 film based in San Francisco, about the fictitious Jejune Institute, of the same name.

9. Samuel Woolley, "Chat Apps: Frontiers and Challenges for Journalism," Institute for the Future, 2018, https://www.iftf.org/partner-with-iftf/research-labs/digital-intelligence-lab/research-archive/chat-apps-frontiers-and-challenges-for-journalism/.

10. Samuel Woolley, *The Reality Game: How the Next Wave of Technology Will Break the Truth* (New York: PublicAffairs, 2020).

11. M. C. Elish and danah boyd, "Situating Methods in the Magic of Big Data and AI," *Communication Monographs* 85, no. 1 (January 2, 2018): 57–80, https://doi.org/10.1080/03637751.2017.1375130; Virginia Eubanks, *Automating Inequality: How High-Tech Tools Profile, Police, and Punish the Poor* (New York: St. Martin's Press, 2017); Sara Wachter-Boettcher, *Technically Wrong: Sexist Apps, Biased Algorithms, and Other Threats of Toxic Tech* (Hoboken, NJ: Norton, 2018).

12. Yochai Benkler, Robert Faris, and Hal Roberts, *Network Propaganda: Manipulation, Disinformation, and Radicalization in American Politics* (New York: Oxford University Press, 2018); Samuel Woolley and Philip Howard, eds., *Computational Propaganda: Political Parties, Politicians, and Political Manipulation on Social Media* (Oxford: Oxford University Press, 2018).

13. Edward S. Herman and Noam Chomsky, *Manufacturing Consent: The Political Economy of the Mass Media* (New York: Pantheon, 2002).

14. Engin Bozdag, "Bias in Algorithmic Filtering and Personalization," *Ethics and Information Technology* 15, no. 3 (September 1, 2013): 209–27, https://doi.org/10.1007/s10676-013-9321-6.

15. Noble, *Algorithms of Oppression*.

16. Eubanks, *Automating Inequality*.

17. Meredith Broussard, *Artificial Unintelligence: How Computers Misunderstand the World* (Cambridge, MA: MIT Press, 2019).

18. Herman and Chomsky, *Manufacturing Consent*, 14.

19. Research has found that the less time people spend on social media, the less depressed and lonely they tend to be. Melissa G. Hunt et al., "No More FOMO: Limiting Social Media Decreases Loneliness and Depression," *Journal of Social and Clinical Psychology* 37, no. 10 (November 8, 2018): 751–68, https://doi.org/10.1521/jscp.2018.37.10.751.

20. Herman and Chomsky, *Manufacturing Consent*, 18.

21. Christopher A. Bail et al., "Exposure to Opposing Views on Social Media Can Increase Political Polarization," *Proceedings of the National Academy of Sciences* 115, no. 37 (2018): 9216, https://doi.org/10.1073/pnas.1804840115; J. K. Lee et al., "Social Media, Network Heterogeneity, and Opinion Polarization," *Journal of Communication* 64, no. 4 (2014): 702–22.

22. Savvas Zannettou et al., "What Is Gab? A Bastion of Free Speech or an Alt-Right Echo Chamber?" in *Companion Proceedings of the Web Conference 2018* (Geneva: International World Wide Web Conferences Steering Committee, 2018), 1007–14.

23. Samuel Woolley, Roya Pakzad, and Nicholas Monaco, "Incubating Hate: Islamophobia and Gab," German Marshall Fund of the United States, June 21, 2019, https://www.gmfus.org/publications/incubating-hate-islamophobia-and-gab.

24. Karen M. Douglas et al., "Understanding Conspiracy Theories," *Political Psychology* 40, no. S1 (2019): 3–35, https://doi.org/10.1111/pops.12568.

25. Greg Rosalsky, "Are Conspiracy Theories Good for Facebook?" *NPR.org*, August 4, 2020, https://www.npr.org/sections/money/2020/08/04/898596655/are-conspiracy-theories-good-for-facebook.

26. Simply put: more traffic and more engagement, even if it's automated or semi-automated, means more money.

27. Benkler, Faris, and Roberts, *Network Propaganda*.

28. Philip N. Howard, *Lie Machines: How to Save Democracy from Troll Armies, Deceitful Robots, Junk News Operations, and Political Operatives* (New Haven, CT: Yale University Press, 2020).

6. Journalism and Political Bots

1. Clifford Geertz, "Deep Hanging Out," *New York Review of Books*, October 22, 1998, 69–72.

2. Edward S. Herman and Noam Chomsky, *Manufacturing Consent: The Political Economy of the Mass Media* (New York: Pantheon, 2002).

3. Ironically, reporters' lack of access, funding, and time is, according to some researchers, caused by social media, which has usurped the news market. D. Wilding et al., "The Impact of Digital Platforms on News and Journalistic Content," University of Technology Sydney, December 7, 2018, https://www.uts.edu.au/sites/default/files/2018-12/CMT%20News%20Report.pdf.

4. Robert M. Faris et al., "Partisanship, Propaganda, and Disinformation: Online Media and the 2016 U.S. Presidential Election," Berkman Klein Center for Internet and Society, 2017, https://dash.harvard.edu/handle/1/33759251.

5. Whitney Phillips, "The Oxygen of Amplification: Better Practices for Reporting on Extremists, Antagonists, and Manipulators," *Data and Society* (Data and Society Research Institute, May 22, 2018), https://datasociety.net/library/oxygen-of-amplification/.

6. Samuel Woolley and Tim Hwang, "Bring on the Bots," *Civicist*, Civic Hall, May 14, 2015, https://civichall.org/civicist/bring-on-the-bots/.

7. Not to be confused with the Irish Republican Army—another IRA with which many readers will be familiar.

8. Kevin Collier and Ken Dilanian, "Russian Internet Trolls Hired U.S. Journalists to Push Their News Website, Facebook Says," *NBC News*, September 1, 2020, https://www.nbcnews.com/tech/tech-news/russian-internet-trolls-hired-u-s-journalists-push-their-news-n1239000.

9. Ibid.

10. Josephine Lukito et al., "The Wolves in Sheep's Clothing: How Russia's Internet Research Agency Tweets Appeared in U.S. News as Vox Populi," *International Journal of Press/Politics* 25, no. 2 (April 1, 2020): 196–216, 197 (quotation), https://doi.org/10.1177/1940161219895215.

11. Samuel Woolley, *Computational Propaganda, Jewish-Americans and the 2018 Midterms: The Amplification of Anti-Semitic Harassment Online* (New York: Anti-Defamation League, 2018), https://www.adl.org/media/12028/download.

12. Joan Donovan, "Americans at Risk: Manipulation and Deception in the Digital Age," testimony before the Committee on Energy and Commerce, 116th Congress (2020), https://www.congress.gov/event/116th-congress/house-event/LC67008/text?loclr=cga-committee.

13. Tasneem Nashrulla, "YouTube Blamed Its 'System' for Letting a Conspiracy Video About a Florida School Shooting Survivor Trend at No. 1," *BuzzFeed News*, February 21, 2018, https://www.buzzfeednews.com/article/tasneemnashrulla/youtube-conspiracy-video-david-hogg.

14. Phillips, "The Oxygen of Amplification."

15. Note: boyd uses lowercase letters for her name.

16. Joan Donovan and danah boyd, "The Case for Quarantining Extremist Ideas," *Guardian*, June 1, 2018, https://www.theguardian.com/commentisfree/2018/jun/01/extremist-ideas-media-coverage-kkk.

17. *Online Harassment of Journalists: Attack of the Trolls* (Paris: Reporters Sans Frontières, 2020), https://rsf.org/sites/default/files/rsf_report_on_online_harassment.pdf.

18. Ibid.

19. Mathew Ingram, "Zoom Under Pressure," *Columbia Journalism Review*, April 2, 2020, https://www.cjr.org/the_media_today/zoom-hackers.php; "WhatsApp Hack Led to Targeting of 100 Journalists and Dissidents," *Financial Times*, October 29, 2019, https://www.ft.com/content/67a5b442-f971-11e9-a354-36acbbb0d9b6.

20. United Nations, "Joint Declaration on Freedom of Expression and 'Fake News,' Disinformation, and Propaganda," March 3, 2017, https://www.osce.org/fom/302796?download=true.

21. Nicholas Monaco, Carly Nyst, and Samuel Woolley, "State-Sponsored Trolling: How Governments Are Deploying Disinformation as Part of Broader Digital Harassment Campaigns," July 19, 2018, https://www.iftf.org/statesponsoredtrolling.

22. Chris Elliott, "The Readers' Editor On . . . Pro-Russian Trolling Below the Line on Ukraine Stories," *Guardian*, May 4, 2014, https://www.theguardian.com/commentisfree/2014/may/04/pro-russia-trolls-ukraine-guardian-online.

23. ADL Task Force on Harassment and Journalism, *Anti-Semitic Targeting of Journalists During the 2016 Presidential Campaign* (New York: Anti-Defamation League, 2016).

24. Julia Angwin, "Cheap Tricks: The Low Cost of Internet Harassment," *ProPublica*, November 9, 2017, https://www.propublica.org/article/cheap-tricks-the-low-cost-of-internet-harassment.

25. Referring to the Saudi crown prince who is suspected of ordering Khashoggi's murder. Chris Bell and Alistair Coleman, "Khashoggi: Bots Feed Saudi Support After Disappearance," *BBC News*, October 18, 2018, https://www.bbc.com/news/blogs-trending-45901584.

26. Alan Crosby, "Suspicions of 'Bots' Grow Over Spikes in 'Dislikes' of Russian Stories Ahead of Election," *Radio Free Europe/Radio Liberty*, February 27, 2018, https://www.rferl.org/a/russia-election-bots-attack-video-dislikes-social-media/29066111.html.

27. President Andrés Manuel López Obrador personally selected them for the position.

28. Steve Fisher, "Mexico Is a Deadly Place to Be a Journalist but Sophisticated Bot Attacks Are Increasing the Danger," *Washington Post*, June 9, 2020, https://www.washingtonpost.com/opinions/2020/06/09/mexico-is-deadly-place-be-journalist-sophisticated-bot-attacks-are-increasing-danger/.

29. Yochai Benkler, Robert Faris, and Hal Roberts, *Network Propaganda: Manipulation, Disinformation, and Radicalization in American Politics* (New York: Oxford University Press, 2018).

30. Joshua A. Tucker et al., "Social Media, Political Polarization, and Political Disinformation: A Review of the Scientific Literature," Hewlett Foundation, March 19, 2018, https://hewlett.org/library/social-media-political-polarization-political-disinformation-review-scientific-literature/.

31. Marc Tuters, Emilija Jokubauskaitė, and Daniel Bach, "Post-Truth Protest: How 4chan Cooked Up the Pizzagate Bullshit," *M/C Journal* 21, no. 3 (August 15, 2018), https://doi.org/10.5204/mcj.1422.

32. Marc Fisher, John Woodrow Cox, and Peter Hermann, "Pizzagate: From Rumor, to Hashtag, to Gunfire in D.C.," *Washington Post*, December 6, 2016, https://www.washingtonpost.com/local/pizzagate-from-rumor-to-hashtag-to-gunfire-in-dc/2016/12/06/4c7def50-bbd4-11e6-94ac-3d324840106c_story.html.

33. Panagiotis Metaxas and Samantha Finn, "Investigating the Infamous #Pizzagate Conspiracy Theory," *Technology Science*, December 17, 2019, https://techscience.org/a/2019121802/.

34. Amanda Robb, "Pizzagate: Anatomy of a Fake News Scandal," *Rolling Stone*, November 16, 2017, https://www.rollingstone.com/feature/anatomy-of-a-fake-news-scandal-125877/.

35. Frederick Schauer, "Fear, Risk and the First Amendment: Unraveling the Chilling Effect," *Boston University Law Review* 58, no. 5 (1978): 685–732.

36. Jon Bruner, "Why 2016 Is Shaping Up to Be the Year of the Bot," *O'Reilly Media*, June 15, 2016, https://www.oreilly.com/radar/why-2016-is-shaping-up-to-be-the-year-of-the-bot/.

37. Kareem Anderson, "Microsoft CEO Satya Nadella Says Chatbots Will Revolutionize Computing," *OnMSFT.Com*, July 11, 2016, https://www.onmsft.com/news/microsoft-ceo-satya-nadella-says-chatbots-will-revolutionize-computing.

38. Philip Bump, "Welcome to the Era of the 'Bot' as Political Boogeyman," *Washington Post*, June 12, 2017, https://www.washingtonpost.com/news/politics/wp/2017/06/12/welcome-to-the-era-of-the-bot-as-political-boogeyman/.

39. John Cifuentes, "Slack Reveals the Next 11 Bot Startups from Its $80 Million Fund," *VentureBeat*, July 19, 2016, https://venturebeat.com/2016/07/19/slack-reveals-the-first-11-bot-startups-from-its-80-million-fund/.

40. Harriet Taylor, "Why Facebook Is Going All in on Chatbots," *CNBC*, April 13, 2016, https://www.cnbc.com/2016/04/13/why-facebook-is-going-all-in-on-chatbots.html.

41. Mai-Hanh Nguyen, "Why the World's Largest Tech Companies Are Building Machine Learning AI Bots Capable of Humanlike Communication," *Business Insider*, November 8, 2017, https://www.businessinsider.com/why-google-microsoft-ibm-tech-companies-investing-chatbots-2017-11.

42. Joseph Lichterman, "For Quartz, Bots Are a Chance to Build a New Path for Interacting with News (and News Outlets)," *Nieman Lab*, March 2, 2017, https://www.niemanlab.org/2017/03/for-quartz-bots-are-a-chance-to-build-a-new-path-for-interacting-with-news-and-news-outlets/.

43. Ross Miller, "AP's 'Robot Journalists' Are Writing Their Own Stories Now," *Verge*, January 29, 2015, https://www.theverge.com/2015/1/29/7939067/ap -journalism-automation-robots-financial-reporting.

44. One example of journalism bots being used before 2016—the year that "chatbot" mania reached its public peak—was the "dreamwriter" bot, which Chinese company Tencent began using in 2015 to churn out "perfect" one-thousand-word business articles through the company's QQ platform. He Huifeng, "End of the Road for Journalists? Tencent's Robot Reporter 'Dreamwriter' Churns Out Perfect 1,000-Word News Story—in 60 Seconds," *South China Morning Post,* September 11, 2015, https://www.scmp.com/tech/china-tech/article/1857196/end-road-journalists -tencents-robot-reporter-dreamwriter-churns-out.

45. "The Washington Post to Use Artificial Intelligence to Cover Nearly 500 Races on Election Day," *Washington Post*, October 19, 2016, https://www.washingtonpost .com/pr/wp/2016/10/19/the-washington-post-uses-artificial-intelligence-to-cover -nearly-500-races-on-election-day/; "4 Lessons BuzzFeed Learned from Using a Bot to Report on Political Conventions," *Poynter*, August 4, 2016, https://www.poynter .org/tech-tools/2016/4-lessons-buzzfeed-learned-from-using-a-bot-to-report-on-the -political-conventions/.

46. Sonya Gee and Prior Flip, "World-First Partnership Between ABC News Bot and Hearken Platform During SA Election," *Australian Broadcasting Corporation*, March 29, 2018, https://www.abc.net.au/news/about/backstory/digital/2018-03-29/ abc-news-bot-and-hearken-curious-platform-during-sa-election/9591966.

47. "Robo-Journalism Gains Traction in Shifting Media Landscape," *France 24* March 10, 2019, https://www.france24.com/en/20190310-robo-journalism-gains -traction-shifting-media-landscape.

48. "Poynter Institute Launches WhatsApp Chatbot to Debunk Coronavirus-Related Hoaxes," *TechCrunch*, May 4, 2020, https://social.techcrunch.com/2020/ 05/04/poynter-institutes-international-fact-checking-network-launches-chatbot-on -whatsapp-to-debunk-thousands-of-coronavirus-related-hoaxes/.

49. Some scholars have argued that bots are useful solely or primarily as information radiators, a form of one-way communication; these scholars argue that tools like bots are best fit to share news online rather than to foster two-way communication. Anders Larsson and Hallvard Moe, "Bots or Journalists? News Sharing on Twitter," *Communications* 40 (November 18, 2014), https://doi.org/10.1515/commun-2015-0014.

50. Samuel Woolley et al., "The Bot Proxy: Designing Automated Self Expression," in *A Networked Self and Platforms, Stories, Connections,* ed. Zizi Papacharissi (New York: Routledge, 2018), 59–76.

51. Hada Sánchez Gonzales and María Sánchez González, "Bots as a News Service and Its Emotional Connection with Audiences. The Case of Politibot," *Doxa Comunicación* 25 (February 1, 2019): 63–84.

52. The authors derived this taxonomy from a sample of extant news bots on Twitter, examining the bots primarily from the point of view of their design. They compare the bots along several axes, including their intent, utility, and functionality. The authors' intent is to guide the future construction of journalism bots by designers and reporting teams. Tetyana Lokot and Nicholas Diakopoulos, "News Bots," *Digital Journalism* 4, no. 6 (August 17, 2016): 682–99, https://doi.org/10.1080/21670811.2015.1081822.

Conclusion

1. Edward S. Herman and Noam Chomsky, *Manufacturing Consent: The Political Economy of the Mass Media* (New York: Pantheon, 2002).

2. Elisabeth Noelle-Neumann, *The Spiral of Silence: Public Opinion—Our Social Skin* (Chicago: University of Chicago Press, 1993).

3. Walter Lippmann, *Public Opinion* (1922; reprint, New York: Simon and Schuster, 1997).

4. Edward L. Bernays, *Crystallizing Public Opinion* (New York: Boni and Liveright, 1923).

5. Edward L. Bernays, *Propaganda* (1928; reprint, New York: Ig, 2005).

6. Jacques Ellul, *Propaganda: The Formation of Men's Attitudes* (New York: Vintage, 1973).

7. L. Neudert, Bence Kollanyi, and Philip N. Howard, "Junk News and Bots During the German Parliamentary Election: What Are German Voters Sharing over Twitter?" Programme on Democracy and Technology, September 19, 2017, https://demtech.oii.ox.ac.uk/research/posts/junk-news-and-bots-during-the-german-parliamentary-election-what-are-german-voters-sharing-over-twitter/; Ensor Jamie, "Swarm of Apparent Twitter Bots Claim Admiration for Winston Peters After Difficult Week," *Newshub*, February 15, 2020, https://www.newshub.co.nz/home/politics/2020/02/swarm-of-apparent-twitter-bots-claim-admiration-of-winston-peters-after-difficult-week.html; Taylor Lorenz, "The Shooter's Manifesto Was Designed to Troll," *The Atlantic*, March 15, 2019, https://www.theatlantic.com/technology/archive/2019/03/the-shooters-manifesto-was-designed-to-troll/585058/.

8. Samantha Bradshaw and Philip N. Howard, *The Global Disinformation Order: 2019 Global Inventory of Organised Social Media Manipulation* (Oxford: Project on Computational Propaganda, 2019).

9. Gary King, Jennifer Pan, and Margaret E. Roberts, "How the Chinese Government Fabricates Social Media Posts for Strategic Distraction, Not Engaged Argument," *American Political Science Review* 3, no. 3 (2017): 484–501.

10. Erkan Saka, "Social Media in Turkey as a Space for Political Battles: AKTrolls and Other Politically Motivated Trolling," *Middle East Critique* 27, no. 2 (April 3, 2018): 161–77, https://doi.org/10.1080/19436149.2018.1439271.

11. Research has shown that these claims are often true. See Samuel Woolley and Douglas Guilbeault, "Computational Propaganda in the United States of America: Manufacturing Consensus Online" (Oxford University Computational Propaganda Project Working Paper Series, No. 2017.5, Oxford, UK, 2017), https://blogs.oii.ox.ac.uk/politicalbots/wp-content/uploads/sites/89/2017/06/Comprop-USA.pdf, and Josephine Lukito et al., "The Wolves in Sheep's Clothing: How Russia's Internet Research Agency Tweets Appeared in U.S. News as Vox Populi," *International Journal of Press/Politics* 25, no. 2 (April 1, 2020): 196–216, https://doi.org/10.1177/1940161219895215.

12. Malcolm Gladwell, "Small Change," *New Yorker,* October 4, 2010, https://www.newyorker.com/magazine/2010/10/04/small-change-malcolm-gladwell.

13. Soroush Vosoughi, Deb Roy, and Sinan Aral, "The Spread of True and False News Online," *Science* 359, no. 6380 (March 9, 2018): 1146–51, https://doi.org/10.1126/science.aap9559.

14. Claire Wardle, "This Video May Not Be Real," *New York Times*, August 14, 2019, https://www.nytimes.com/2019/08/14/opinion/deepfakes-adele-disinformation.html; James Vincent, "An Online Propaganda Campaign Used AI-Generated Headshots to Create Fake Journalists," *Verge*, July 7, 2020, https://www.theverge.com/2020/7/7/21315861/ai-generated-headshots-profile-pictures-fake-journalists-daily-beast-investigation.

15. Ronald J. Diebert, "The Road to Digital Unfreedom: Three Painful Truths About Social Media," *Journal of Democracy* 30, no. 1 (January 2019): 25–39.

16. Yochai Benkler, *The Wealth of Networks: How Social Production Transforms Markets and Freedom* (New Haven, CT: Yale University Press, 2007); Taylor Owen, *Disruptive Power: The Crisis of the State in the Digital Age* (Oxford: Oxford University Press, 2015).

17. David Karpf, *The MoveOn Effect: The Unexpected Transformation of American Political Advocacy* (New York: Oxford University Press, 2012).

18. Daniel Kreiss, *Prototype Politics: Technology-Intensive Campaigning and the Data of Democracy* (New York: Oxford University Press, 2016).

19. Jennifer Stromer-Galley, *Presidential Campaigning in the Internet Age* (New York: Oxford University Press, 2014).

20. Eitan D. Hersh, *Hacking the Electorate: How Campaigns Perceive Voters* (New York: Cambridge University Press, 2015).

21. Jacob Gursky and Samuel Woolley, "The Trump 2020 App Is a Voter Surveillance Tool of Extraordinary Power," *MIT Technology Review,* June 21, 2020, https://www.technologyreview.com/2020/06/21/1004228/trumps-data-hungry-invasive-app-is-a-voter-surveillance-tool-of-extraordinary-scope/.

22. Andrew Chadwick, *The Hybrid Media System: Politics and Power* (Oxford: Oxford University Press, 2013).

23. Karpf, *The MoveOn Effect,* 10.

24. Christopher Paul and Miriam Matthews, "The Russian 'Firehose of Falsehood' Propaganda Model," RAND Corporation, July 11, 2016, https://www.rand.org/pubs/perspectives/PE198.html.

25. Taina Bucher, *If . . . Then: Algorithmic Power and Politics* (New York: Oxford University Press, 2018).

26. Tarlton Gillespie, "Can an Algorithm Be Wrong? Twitter Trends, the Specter of Censorship, and Our Faith in the Algorithms Around Us," Culture Digitally, 2011, http://culturedigitally.org/2011/10/can-an-algorithm-be-wrong/.

27. Tarleton Gillespie, "The Relevance of Algorithms," in *Media Technologies: Essays on Communication, Materiality, and Society,* ed. Tarleton Gillespie, Pablo J. Boczkowski, and Kirsten A. Foot (Cambridge, MA: MIT Press, 2014), 167.

28. Philip Howard, Samuel Woolley, and Ryan Calo, "Algorithms, Bots, and Political Communication in the US 2016 Election: The Challenge of Automated Political Communication for Election Law and Administration," *Journal of Information Technology and Politics* 15 (April 11, 2018): 1–13, https://doi.org/10.1080/19331681.2018.1448735.

29. Samuel Woolley, *The Reality Game: How the Next Wave of Technology Will Break the Truth* (New York: PublicAffairs, 2020).

30. Ann M. Ravel, Samuel C. Woolley, and Hamsini Sridharan, "Principles and Policies to Counter Deceptive Digital Politics," MapLight and the Institute for the Future, February 11, 2019, https://www.iftf.org/future-now/article-detail/new-policy-platform-outlines-solutions-to-address-deceptive-digital-politics/.

31. Howard, Woolley, and Calo, "Algorithms, Bots, and Political Communication in the US 2016 Election."

32. Trushar Barot and Eytan Oren, "Guide to Chat Apps," Tow Center for Digital Journalism, November 9, 2015, https://www.cjr.org/tow_center_reports/guide_to_chat_apps.php/.

33. Samuel Woolley and Katie Joseff, "Demand for Deceit: How the Way We Think Drives Disinformation," International Forum for Democratic Studies, January 8, 2020, https://www.ned.org/demand-for-deceit-how-way-we-think-drives-disinformation-samuel-woolley-katie-joseff/.

34. Jay Sullivan, "Introducing a Forwarding Limit on Messenger," About, Meta, September 3, 2020, https://about.fb.com/news/2020/09/introducing-a-forwarding-limit-on-messenger/.

35. Facebook has said it will adopt end-to-end encryption across all of its social media tools.

36. Jonathan Albright, "The Graph API: Key Points in the Facebook and Cambridge Analytica Debacle," *Medium*, March 21, 2018, https://medium.com/tow-center/the-graph-api-key-points-in-the-facebook-and-cambridge-analytica-debacle-b69fe692d747.

37. Sabrina Rodriguez and Marc Caputo, "'This Is F---ing Crazy': Florida Latinos Swamped by Wild Conspiracy Theories," *Politico*, September 14, 2020, https://www.politico.com/news/2020/09/14/florida-latinos-disinformation-413923.

38. Audie Cornish and Heidi Schlumpf, "How Political Campaigns Are Using 'Geofencing' Technology to Target Catholics at Mass," *NPR.org*, February 6, 2020, https://www.npr.org/2020/02/06/803508851/how-political-campaigns-are-using-geofencing-technology-to-target-catholics-at-m.

39. Gursky and Woolley, "The Trump 2020 App Is a Voter Surveillance Tool of Extraordinary Power."

Index